Essential Series

C000121342

Springer

London
Berlin
Heidelberg
New York
Barcelona
Budapest
Hong Kong
Milan
Paris
Santa Clara
Singapore
Tokyo

Duncan Reed and Peter Thomas

Essential
HTML *fast*

 Springer

Duncan Reed, BSc (Hons)
Peter J. Thomas BA(Hons), PhD, MErgS, MIEE, Ceng, MBCS, FRSA
Centre for Personal Information Management
University of the West of England, Frenchay Campus,
Coldharbour Lane, Bristol BS16 1QY, UK

Series Editor
John Cowell, BSc (Hons), MPhil, PhD
Department of Computer and Information Sciences
De Montfort University, Kents Hill Campus,
Hammerwood Gate, Kents Hill, Milton Keynes, MK7 6HP, UK

ISBN 3-540-76199-3 Springer-Verlag Berlin Heidelberg New York

British Library Cataloguing in Publication Data
A catalogue record for this book is available from the British Library.

Library of Congress Cataloging-in-Publication Data
Reed, Duncan. 1971-
    Essential HTML fast / Duncan Reed and Peter Thomas
        p.   cm. - - (Essential series)
    Includes index.
    ISBN 3-540-76199-3 (pbk. : alk. paper)
    1. HTML (Document markup language) I. Thomas, Peter. II. Title. III. Series: Essential
    series (Springer-Verlag)
QA76.76.H94R44 1997
005.7'2--DC21   97-29237

© Springer-Verlag London Limited 1998
Printed in Great Britain

Typesetting: Camera ready by author
Printed and bound at the Athenæum Press Ltd., Gateshead, Tyne and Wear
34/3830-543210 Printed on acid-free paper

Contents

1 INTRODUCTION 1

Introduction 1
Why use the Web? 2
Who should read this book 3
Assumptions made in this book 3
Things you'll need 4
How to use the book 4
Some Internet and World Wide Web concepts and terms 4
    Clients and Servers 6
    IP addresses and URLs 6
    The Hypertext Transfer Protocol 7
Browsers 8
    How to get the browser 8
Other tools 9
    HTML editors 9
Graphics Software 9

2 PLANNING AND DESIGNING YOUR WEB SITE 10

Introduction 10
Planning ahead 11
A simple project plan: Wallace's nuts, bolts and grommets 11
    Company background 11
    Define the market 11
    Define the mission 11
    Define the vision 11
    Define the strategy 12
    Analyse the business 12
Starting small and working up 13
Making use of Hypertext 14
Designing the site 14
    Consistency 14
    Identity 15
    Navigation 15
    What makes a 'good' web site? 16

3   EARLY HTML: YOUR FIRST HOME PAGE 19

Introduction 19
Getting started: the browser 19
Your first home page 21
Head, body and foot 22
What it all means 22
    The <HEAD> and </HEAD> tags 23
    The <BODY> tag 23
How to do more interesting things 24
Commonly used tags 24
Using different sized headings; the <H> tags 24
    The <P> tag 25
    The <DIV> tag 26
    The <BR> tag 28
    The <HR> tag 29
Structuring your documents 29
Coda 30

4   LINKS AND HYPERTEXT 31

Introduction 31
More about Hypertext 32
Creating Links 32
Links to external documents 33
Creating links within the same document 34
The Soccer Web 35
Making it into a 'proper' web 38
    Relative referencing: links to other files on your server 38
    Accessing other forms of information 39
Coda 39

5 LOGICAL AND PHYSICAL MARK-UP 41

Introduction 41
Use Logical Mark-up! 42
More logical mark-up 43
    <CITE> 43
    <DFN> 43
    <STRONG> 44
    <CODE> 44
    <INS> and <DEL> 45
Physical Mark-up 45
    <I> and <B> 46
    <TT> 46

<BIG> and <SMALL> 46
<SUB> and <SUP> 46
   An example of various physical mark-up tags 46
Coda 48

6 USING IMAGES **49**
Introduction 49
Using images 50
GIFS, JPEGS and PNG: types of images for the web 50
   GIFS 50
   Types of GIFs 50
   Interlaced GIFs 51
   When to use GIFs 51
JPEGs 51
   Progressive JPEGs 51
   When to use JPEGs 51
Including images in your pages; the <IMG> tag 51
Alternate text 52
Moving your images left, right and centre 53
The Align attribute 53
The Height and Width attributes 55
HSPACE and VSPACE 56
Borders 57
Client side image maps 58
   Creating a map using the <OBJECT> tag 59
Button bars 59

7 LISTS **61**
Introduction 61
Unordered lists 61
   Using the type attribute 62
Ordered Lists 63
   Attributes for Ordered Lists 63
   Type 63
   Using start and value 65
   The <LI> tag 66
   Setting values arbitrarily 68
Nested Lists 69
   Unordered lists 70
   Ordered lists 70
Definition Lists: DL, DT and DD 71
   72

8   FORMS **75**

Introduction 75
Form basics 75
How forms are handled: CGI 76
Defining the form 76
Form methods 77
   The GET method 77
   The POST method 77
Sending a form through e-mail 77
The <INPUT> tag 78
   Text fields 78
   Text Areas 79
   Creating Submit and Reset Buttons 80
Checkboxes and radio buttons 81
Radio Buttons 83
Drop down menus and scrolling lists 83
   Drop down menus 84
   Scrolling List Boxes 85
   Coda 87

9   FRAMES **89**

Introduction 89
Designing the Pages 90
Proceed with Caution 90
Frame Tags 91
   Frameset and its attributes 92
   Rows and Columns 92
   Nesting frames 93
   NORESIZE 95
   Scrolling frames 95
   Frame borders 95
   <NOFRAMES> 95
Using Frames effectively 96
   The TARGET="_top" attribute 96

10 TABLES **97**

Introduction 97
The <TABLE> tag 98
   Adding columns 99
   Captions 99
   Table headers versus data 101
Borders, spacing and padding 102

Adding a border 102
Spacing 102
Padding 104
Combining all three 104
More complex table layout 105
Text alignment in tables 105
Spanning rows and columns 108
Adding colour 109
Coda 110

11 CASCADING STYLE SHEETS 111

Introduction 111
Cascading Style Sheets 112
Designing your site for style sheets 112
How style sheets work 112
Inheritance 113
Context 114
Multiple Selectors 114
Classes 115
Defining generic classes 115
Pseudo-classes 116
Properties 117
Text properties 117
The text-indent property 117
The text-align property 118
The line-height property 118
Font properties 119
Colors and background properties 119
Linking your style sheets to the documents 120
Including style definitions in the head of your document 120
Linking the style sheets in 120
Importing styles 121
Why you should use style sheets 121

12 WEB TECHNOLOGIES 123

Introduction 123
Multimedia 123
Files sizes 124
Plug-ins 124
Helper applications 124
Using the <OBJECT> tag to include multimedia 125
The Common Gateway Interface 125
Creating interactivity: programming on the web 126

Perl 126
Java 127
JavaScript 127
Web resources 129
    Search Engines 129
    The World Wide Web consortium 129

INDEX **131**

1

Introduction

Introduction

One of the most often-repeated questions of recent years is 'Are you on the Web?'

The growth of the World Wide Web (WWW or simply 'Web') has been phenomenal. It seems that everyone has a web site, or is at least planning have one, and everyone wants to get on-line with their products and services, accounts of their favourite hobbies, their resumes, or pictures of their loved ones.

So that you too can join in the on-line revolution, this book will help you get onto the web: to make informed decisions about developing your own web site, how to plan and design the site, and then how to get the site on-line for the world to see.

Why use the Web?

There are many reasons why you would want to use the Web, and why the web is becoming an essential tool for business. Some of these are:

- **It is cross-platform:** If you're reading this at work, you're probably painfully aware of some of the problems caused by being tied to a particular type of computer. You might have come across some software that would make your job easier, but then discover that the software is only available for a different computer running a different operating system. You may have been sent some documents by a client which you subsequently discover you can't read, as the disk seems to be of the wrong type. For those of us who use computers in our work these problems are all-too familiar. Some of these problems can be avoided by using the Web and its associated technologies. For information providers, the web is invaluable because any computer system, using any operating system, can be used to access the same information as everyone else.

- **Providing information is simple:** Providing information through the Web is straightforward. You can start in a very simple manner and then build up your web site as you gain more experience. Unlike many computer technologies, the web is something that almost anyone can get to grips with. For business users, it will come as a refreshing change to not have to immediately employ a consultant to get things running (although there are Web design consultancies appearing). This book will equip you with the skills to produce a professional and effective web site.

- **It is ubiquitous:** Although the web is a very young technology—it wasn't until late 1994 that it really took off—it is now ubiquitous. The number of web sites has grown from a few hundred University-based sites to several hundred thousand sites of all kinds—business, academic, and personal. For business users the Web is a new marketing channel to reach current and future customers all over the world. For academic institutions there is the opportunity to attract a more diverse range of students and to become more accessible to the community. Personal users can reach people all over the world with similar interests. Statistics on the growth of the web are hard to pin down—such is the rate of growth that by the time statistics are published they are out of date. However, it would be accurate to say that there are several **billion** individual web pages, **with several hundred thousand** web sites.

Who should read this book

This book is aimed at a range of readers with a wide range of skills and knowledge. Like other books in this series the aim is to give readers a quick 'on-ramp' to knowledge and skills in a practical, hands-on way. Books in this series are also intended to be accessible desk references which readers can turn to for specific advice.

We certainly don't intend this book to be exhaustive—we want you to learn quickly and to be spared having to plough through hundreds of pages of detail searching for what you want. The book is intended to help you understand how to:

- apply effective techniques for the design of extensible professional web sites;
- make your web site accessible to everyone, through the effective use of HTML (the HyperText Markup Language)—the language used to develop web pages and sites.

So, the intended readers for this book are:

- business users who want to develop professional-standard web pages with the minimum of fuss;
- students taking a course on HTML and the Web;
- personal users who want to learn more about just what it is that they are surfing through;.
- more experienced users who still need prompts and reminders from time to time.

Assumptions made in this book

In order for you to get the most from this book, we need to make a few assumptions about you, the reader. If you're an absolute computer novice then this book can still be a lot of use to you. We would suggest however, that you first read something about the Internet and World Wide Web: most computing magazines contain excellent information. We will briefly review the very basic terminology and concepts, but we assume some basic knowledge, for example we assume:

- you have seen and used the Web: have browsed pages and sites and have a grasp of what the Internet and the World Wide Web is and does;
- that you are a reasonably competent computer user: you are familiar starting up and closing down applications and installing new software on your machine;

- that you already have a connection to the Internet: either via a modem through an ISP (Internet Service Provider) or, if you are a business user, access via your company network.

Things you'll need

Writing HTML and putting together web pages is in itself not particularly taxing of computing resources—another blessing of the Web is that you aren't required to have the very latest upgraded multimedia personal computer to design and access Web sites.

There are no platform restrictions (as we noted earlier the Web is cross-platform), but as a basic guideline we would advise a minimum of:

- PC—80486dx4 or better
- Mac—608030 or better

For both Mac and PC, a minimum of 16Mbtyes of RAM is usually required, and around 50Mb of spare hard disk space is recommended (these requirements are usually standard for most new computers). If you're using a UNIX system, then you really shouldn't need to worry too much about system resources—merely check to see that you have enough hard disk space.

How to use the book

The book has been designed so that you can read it cover to cover, and the examples are arranged in order of increasing complexity and sophistication. However, once you have a grasp of the basic requirements for HTML and you have specific things you wish to do, you can also dip into the book and get what you want quickly.

The book does not cover **everything** about the Web, which would make the book twice the size, and twice as hard to read (there are lots of Very Big Web Books lying unread on the shelves of your bookstore and we don't want ours to join them).

To use the book just follow the examples and give it a try. One of the advantages of HTML is that you can produce results very quickly.

Some Internet and World Wide Web concepts and terms

Inevitably there is some computing terminology to learn. This is both so that you can understand other more complex concepts and terms relating to the web, and also crucial in allowing you to impress your friends at parties (or at least the parties we go to).

We assume that you understand what the following terms and concepts mean, but we will just quickly clarify them before we move on:

- **World-Wide Web** (WWW or Web): a way of making available information (often called, in this context, **content**) from computers so that anyone who knows where it is located (and is allowed to access it) can view it;

- **Web Page** (or simply **page**): the way that the world wide web content is designed and displayed; authors put their content into pages (like pages of a book) which readers can view via their own computer; pages contain images, text and (as we will see later) sounds and moving images in the form of video clips or animations;

- **HTML**: the HyperText Markup Language, a computer language for developing Web pages. HTML allows the author to control (amongst other things) the colour, size and style of any text, the size and positioning of images, and the links between different elements of a web page or elements of a web site. HTML allows authors to control how their content will be viewed by the readers who access their web sites by writing files of HTML instructions known as **tags** which in detail specify the way the document is intended to look. (The HTML examples in this book will be shown in an arial font, and for the sake of brevity the standard opening and closing tags required by HTML will not be written out each time).

- **Web site** (or simply **site**): a collection of web pages, written in HTML, gathered together on a single computer and linked together.

- **Internet**: the terms 'Internet' and 'World Wide Web' are often taken to mean the same thing, when in fact, they are not. The Internet is simply a collection of computers around the world, all connected together to form a gigantic network (using, amongst other means, the public telephone system, dedicated computer networks and satellites). Figure 1.1 illustrates the Internet and how a web page is requested.

What this network does is to allow the World Wide Web (and other systems such as **email**) to be used to access content on many computers. Conversely, content can be specifically designed for use on the Web (as we will see in this book), but it is also available from various other sources that are not designed solely for use on the Web (such as **ftp**—or file transfer protocol—which is a very fast way of tranferring content between computers).

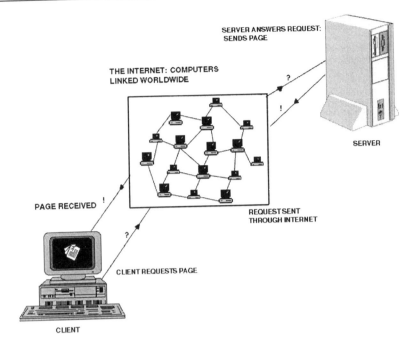

Figure 1.1: Requesting a web page over the Internet.

Clients and Servers

When you're accessing content on the Internet, you request documents from a **server**, using a **client**. You can view this as a kind of shopping: you make a request for something as a client; the server checks to see if it has what you requested, and if it does, it serves it to you.

On the World Wide Web, computers which deliver content to your computer are called **web servers**, and the client software making the request from your own computer is called a **browser**.

The browser is really a convenient way of accessing content without having to know much more than where you want to go. Browsers allow you to specify what content you want and from where, and will get it for you, delivering it for you to view. Browsers can also be used to write your own Web pages in HTML (see below).

IP addresses and URLs

To connect a computer to the Internet and have it do anything useful, it must have a unique address so that all the other computers on the Internet know where it is. This address, unsurprisingly, takes the form of a number.

The format of these numbers is described by the **Internet Protocol** and consists of a group of numbers which look like: **127.0.0.1**. Each of the four numbers is joined to the other by periods, and each of the numbers is never bigger than 255. The unique number assigned to a particular computer is called an **IP address**. You won't have to worry too much about IP addresses unless you are setting up your own web server.

Numbers are great for computers but they tend to make most people's heads hurt. Fortunately, there is a mechanism for giving computers on the Internet a 'proper' name. On the web, these names are known as **Uniform Resource Locators**, or **URLs**. So, while your machine may have the IP address **123.234.56.78**, it will probably be known to you as **www.atestserver.com**.

While IP numbers are always in the same format, the names we give computers are different which gives us some clues as to the kind of content we might find on that site.

For example, the publishers of this book, Springer-Verlag London, have a web site that has the URL **www.svl.co.uk**. This tells us several things; the computer at Springer is a web server, whose name is **www**. The **svl** part is simply the initials of the company. The two suffixes tell us that the site is a company (**.co**) based in the UK (**.uk**). There are several suffixes which give information about the type of site. For example, there are **.gov**, **.com** and **.org** sites: these denote government, commercial, and non-profit organisation sites, respectively.

The URL doesn't also specify the name of the computer, but can also specify the Web page that you might be looking for. Most people will access documents by requesting their browser (often called **pointing their browser**) to get content from a particular computer which contains a Web site such as **www.atestserver.com,** but it is also possible to request to view a specific document, say **index.html**, by asking the browser to access it using the complete URL **www.atestserver.com/index.html**. The convention is that all Web pages are distinguished from other forms of content by having the suffix **.html** (or occasionally **.htm**) attached to them.

The Hypertext Transfer Protocol

Finally, **HTTP** (HyperText Transfer Protocol) is the way that most documents on the web are transmitted. Basically the protocol bundles up the requested information into a standard format that is then decoded by the browser which made the request.

By convention, requests from browsers start with the letters **http://** (you don't need to know why) and are followed by the URL (an IP address or the name of a computer somewhere on the Internet).

So, most requests for content on the Internet look like this:

http://127.0.0.1/index.html

or

http://www.atestserver.com/index.html

Most written addresses will look like this (most are usually longer) and all that is required is to type the address into the address box in your browser and you will be able to access the site.

Browsers

HTML pages can be written using any straightforward text editor (usually known as **hand coding**) but you need to be able to look at your pages through the various stages of their development, and indeed when you have made the pages available on the web. This is a process of prototyping your pages—writing the HTML to construct the page and then testing whether it looks like, and does, what you want.

The software you will need to view completed and under-construction pages is a browser. Some browsers also allow you construct HTML pages using editing tools embedded within them.

At present, a battle is being fought in the browser world between the two major players; Netscape Communications Corporation, and Microsoft Corporation. The Netscape browser is called **Netscape Navigator**, and Microsoft's product is called **Internet Explorer**. These are the two most widely used Web browsers and between them account for 98% of the browsers being run on computers around the world today.

- **Netscape Navigator** is available for the following operating systems: MS windows 3.x, 95 and NT, Macintosh 6080x0 and PowerPC, OS/2 Warp, SunOs4.1, AIX, SGI Irix 5.3 and 6.2, Linux
- **Internet Explorer** is available for: MS windows 3.x, 95, NT and MacOS

There is not, we suggest, too much to choose between the two browsers. One caveat though: depending on which browser you choose, there may be a charge. Microsoft's Internet Explorer is currently free, and if you are using Netscape Navigator for academic use it is also free. However, if you are using it in your business you will have to buy it. You will need to check at the Netscape and Microsoft Web sites for changes in these policies.

Through the course of this book, all the examples shown will be on a version of the Netscape Navigator.

How to get the browser

The normal place to get a copy of a browser is from the Web site of the browser developer.

If you plan to do some of your development work on a standalone PC or Mac (perhaps at home), we would suggest you check out one of the many PC or Mac computing magazines. Most of these publications come with free CDs which often contain a latest release of either of the two browsers.

If you're on a network as a business or academic user, your first port of call should be your network supervisor. Ask them if they can obtain and install the browser for you.

The browsers can be downloaded from:

- Netscape Communications   **http://home.netscape.com/**
- Microsoft   **http://www.microsoft.com/**

Other tools

HTML editors

There are a multitude of editing tools around to help people develop HTML pages and web sites. Their capabilities and requirements are incredibly varied, and in the several years we have been developing web sites we have not come across a single tool which is entirely up to scratch. Many tools help the user with simple tasks, and when things become a little more tricky fail to help. In the course of developing a web site you will almost always need to 'hand code' at least some of it. To be able to do that, you need to understand what HTML is and how it works.

There isn't one standard web-writing tool for all platforms, so our policy in this book is to keep it simple. All of the examples in this book have been hand coded on a simple text editor.

Having said that, we don't see any problem with using such tools if you find one to meet your own requirements.

Furthermore, the ethos of the Web is one of community and egalitarianism: with a little knowledge and common sense, just about anyone can produce good web pages. With some patience and a little flair, you can make your home web site have as much style and impact as one which has been professionally designed.

Graphics Software

You'll also need some method of editing, creating and altering graphics and images you want to display on your web pages. Once again, there are a great many tools around. If you have some money to spare, we recommend obtaining a copy of **Photoshop**; it is available for PC, Mac and Unix systems, and is the *de facto* standard for handling graphics. There are cheaper, often freeware and shareware, options such as **Paintshop Pro** (for Windows 3.1 and 95). Hunt through your computing magazine's free CD since there is often a shareware graphics program which will suit your needs perfectly.

2

Planning and Designing your Web site

Introduction

The explanations and examples throughout this book will give you the skills to develop an excellent website. With a little forethought and some planning, you can make your web site look as cool as any of the best sites on the web.

When you surf the web (now that you have your browser working, and Internet connection all sorted out) you will see sites which seem to be disjointed, illogical and hard to follow. It doesn't need to be like that. By applying a few simple principles, you can have an easy to navigate, consistent, and easy to maintain and simple to extend web site.

In this chapter you will learn the importance of:

- Planning ahead
- Starting small and working up
- Making use of hypertext
- Designing the site

Planning ahead

When you begin to consider putting a web site together you will quickly recognise that you should plan and design your web site in exactly the same way as you would with any other product. This will be obvious for those of you in business, but we suggest that it makes sense to plan and design any web site. As a home user, you may be considering putting a site together because you feel you have something interesting to tell the rest of the world, and it still makes sense to make your site as accessible and easy to use as possible.

When you are planning any project several questions arise—and they are the same questions regardless of who you are—business, home user or student. What follows is a very simple example project plan and subsequent site design for the fictional company *Wallace's Nuts, Bolts and Grommets* (or simply *Wallace's*).

A simple project plan: Wallace's nuts, bolts and grommets

Company background

The company produces a wide range of nuts, bolts, screws and other semi-permanent fixings. The company has several factories around the country each producing a particular type of nut or bolt and several sales offices and distribution centres close to the factories. The Managing Director, Ms Wallace, is becoming increasingly aware of the increasing costs of creating and distributing marketing materials. She discovers that most of the company's clients have access to the Internet, and thus makes the decision to investigate the feasibility of producing a web site.

Define the market

The first step in the project is to understand what kinds of content potential users of the site will need to have access to in order to understand the company's products and services. In the case of *Wallace's* the prime audience is existing customers, but Ms Wallace is keen to see if the site can attract new customers.

Define the mission

The next step is to define a mission statement, which describes the outcomes *Wallace's* want to achieve on-line. This statement might look like this:

'The mission of Wallace's Nuts, Bolts and Grommets' web site is to provide clear, precise and up to date information on all areas of our business to our existing customers in order to maximise the pre- and post-sales services available to those customers.'

Define the vision

Ms. Wallace is really keen to keep her customers happy and so her vision for the web site is:

'The WNBG web site will be recognised by the customers as being a permanently available, high quality information source for all aspects of nuts, bolts and grommets.'

Define the strategy

In order to meet the requirements of the mission statement and Ms. Wallace's vision, the WNBG web site should

- provide high quality information to the customer
- it should do this in a simple, straightforward manner
- the site should be easy to interact with
- it should be regularly updated
- it should provide the opportunity for feedback from the customer.

Analyse the business

Now we have some a more complete view of what the site is to achieve, specific requirements for actually designing the site can be developed. The first is to more precisely **analyse the business** and the **business processes** for which the site is to be developed.

If the aim of the site is to provide additional service to customers, it naturally makes sense to analyse the business processes and organisation in order to figure out where use of web-based information can add something of value to the customer's relationship with the company. For Wallace's this might be:

Step 1: List the areas of operation for the business

Manufacturing
    Nuts
    Bolts
    Screws

Bespoke contracts

Sales
Mobile Sales team
Sales office
Conferences/Trade fairs

Distribution
Regional Offices
Haulage contractors

Customer Service
Regional office
Head office

Step 2: Work through the business process

Sales team completes contract
Customer calls in to check details
Order goes to manufacturing
Products made and packed
Distribution delivers products

Although this is a very simplistic business process, you should be able to see that breaking things down in this way should help identify who needs what kind of information, why they need it and what use they will make of it.

From this you can also see that it would make sense for *Wallace's* to break down the web site into four main components:

- sales
- manufacturing
- distribution
- customer service.

Each of the components might have specific pages, or specific sets of pages, all tied to a single 'front page' (or **home page**) which describes the company and its operations.

Starting small and working up

Leaving Ms. Wallace to develop the company's Web site, we can now go on to understand some of the more detailed features of a web site.

As we said in chapter 1, the best web sites provide **relevant information**, displayed **clearly** and **simply**. Users will come to a site with specific information needs and requirements—especially in the case of Wallace's site, users are unlikely to be simply surfing for fun.

This means that you must match the design and content of the site to what you would like to achieve, and introduces one of the most beneficial features of the Web and Web-based content: the ability to links things together. This is known as **hypertext**.

Making use of Hypertext

What makes the web such a powerful (and often frustrating) information resource is its **hypertext** capabilities. Hypertext means that you can link one Web page with others (even Web pages at other sites hosted on other computers) so that when they are selected by a viewer, the viewer can zip between them.

This is done by placing **hypertext links** within Web pages. In the case of *Wallaces'* Web site, we have seen that all areas of the business can be linked together at the highest level as functions of the company, and there will also be links between, for example, the sales department and customer services.

Using hypertext, you and visitors to the site can leap from one page to another. We will be dealing with the topic of linking in greater detail in **chapter 4.**

Designing the site

When one of us first started working on web-oriented products, the particular company had around ten web pages accessible by the outside world. That was in late 1994. Now that same company has several hundred Web pages, with links to several thousand documents.

This *always* happens. *Without fail.*

Your web site will always grow. Furthermore, the amount of information you are trying to cram into your home page will also always grow. Bearing that in mind, our first rule for Web page design is

Keep it *simple*

Consistency

An aim in designing your Web site should be to make accessing it and viewing the content it contains as simple, easy and clear as possible.

One of the key elements to designing a web site is therefore **consistency**. You should ensure that the different areas of your web site have their own identity, but remain clearly part of the whole site. In designing a site, you will have a fairly strong idea (or you should by now) of what content you are going to use. The content should lead you to make decisions about what kind of material you are going to need on *every* page.

Identity

Creating an **identity** for your web site is all about perception: what kind of perceptions do you wish visitors to have of your web site (and so of you)? Many businesses attempt to make their web sites look exactly the same as their paper-based marketing material with its corporate 'branding'. Usually these sites are visually well-presented, but have little engaging content; visitors tend not to stay or come back very often.

We believe that visitor's perceptions of your company or you will be more heavily influenced by **content** than by **style**. However, using graphic images and standard devices used in other areas of your business allows you to create a recognisable web identity, and helps to make your site consistent.

Navigation

When you start to harness the power of hypertext, you will quickly realise how bewilderingly complex things can get. It is incredibly easy to get lost in a web site; you follow a link, and then can't remember where you were, or indeed why you decided to follow that link.

Although there is no way of actually guaranteeing that some foolish visitor will not get lost, the following suggestions will help ensure that almost all of your users will know where they are most of the time.

- Analyse the content: it is essential that you think carefully about the content of the site in a detailed fashion, asking questions like: **what do I want the reader to understand from this page and what will they probably want to read next? In what order do I want visitors to view the content?** and **Do I need text or images here to convey what I want?** There are no hard-and-fast set of rules to help you do this, and the little research that has been done on the ways visitors navigate web sites doesn't help too much. Most sites provide features such as **navigation bars** which allow the visitor to go backwards and forwards, and **informative titles** for pages. Beyond this it is a matter of trial and error.
- Prototype the site: **prototyping** simply means designing and redesigning the site. HTML allows you to have successive versions of your web pages, which become more and more complete until you have a well-designed site. It is a good idea to have prototyped the entire site—the content, the navigation routes through the site, any multimedia elements such as graphics, video and sound—before you can consider it finished; any changes you make as you refine and update the site should also be prototyped.

Then, when you are happy with the result

- **go on-line:** getting the site to go on-line and live is done by transferring your pages onto a server with a URL which can be accessed via the Internet. Although you will probably prototype your pages on your own PC for public access the pages must be 'mounted' on a server. Either your Internet Service Provider (**ISP**) may provide a personal Web page area for you to mount your pages (and provide tools to do so), or if you are on a company Internet, the administrator of the Web site (often grandly called the **webmaster**) will do this for you.

What makes a 'good' web site?

There is no one answer to 'what makes a good web site?' We have discussed some of the qualities—clear navigation, interesting content, a consistent design, and a site which conveys a strong sense of identity. Beyond that it is hard to pin down what a good web site is.

A good site might have excellent graphic design qualities, interesting content and good navigation features but fails somehow to capture the imagination—it might just not be cool enough. Or, a good site might have the latest multimedia elements, use new technologies (such as video, audio or animated images) but still not quite be what visitors would like to see—it doesn't engage them.

One thing visitors **do** want of many sites however is **changing content**: sites should be updated regularly and appropriately to ensure they visitors come back and come back often. What little research that has been done on trying to understand what the factors are that determine whether a web site design is good or not is inconclusive, but common sense tells us that visitors are unlikely to come back time and time again if all they see is the same thing.

That part is up to you, and how often you choose to update your site. What we will do in the remainder of this book is to give you an understanding of the tools and techniques to enable you to develop and manage your web site so that your visitors **do** come back time and time again.

3

Early HTML: your first home page

Introduction

In this chapter, you will get to grips with the simple structure of HTML, learn some of its requirements, and learn to use some of the most common tags. You'll also learn to:

- Get your browser running;
- Make your first HTML page;
- See it on your browser (exciting!);
- Use basic tags of HTML.

Getting started: the browser

Now you have your web browser, your graphics program and your text editor. At this point you don't even need to be on the Internet. All your HTML pages will be saved to your hard disk and the browser will have no problem accessing them from there

When you installed your browser, an icon like this appeared on your desktop.

To get the browser started, simply double-click on it, and the initial browser window will appear on your screen. What may happen next is that you'll get an alert box something like this (figure 3.1).

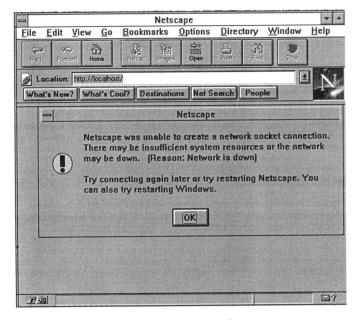

Figure 3.1: Browser network error.

This is because by default, Netscape opens up and immediately starts searching for the Netscape web site. If you're not actually connected to the Internet this will not happen. If you are, getting access to Netscape's home page can take a while, because everyone is connecting to their site to see what Netscape are up to right now.

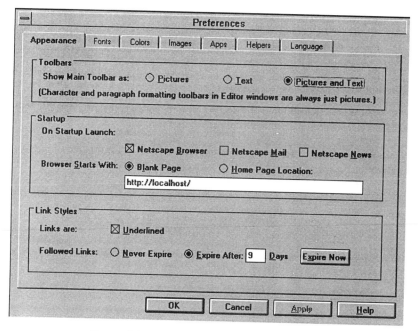

Figure 3.2: Setting the browser start page.

To avoid this every time you start the Netscape browser, follow these steps.

Double click on the Netscape icon to get the browser started

- Click on the **Options** menu
- Click on General preferences

Where it says 'Browser starts with'

- Click on **Blank page**
- Click **OK**

Next time you start the browser, it won't start trying to make any network connections and will start with an empty window.

Your first home page

In the next ten minutes or so, you will have created your first HTML page.

- Open up your text editing program;
- Create a new document;
- Call it '*Myhome.html*'

When you save the document, make sure that the **document format** option in your text editor is set to 'text file', 'ASCII text' or something similar. Also make sure that the *.html* extension is attached to the file name, otherwise your browser may have a hard time reading the file.

Head, body and foot

All HTML documents have a similar structure. The structure always has a **HEAD**, **BODY** and **FOOT**.

The simplest HTML documents will look like this

```
<!DOCTYPE HTML PUBLIC "-//W3C//DTD HTML 3.2//EN">
<HEAD>
<TITLE>My first home page</TITLE>
</HEAD>
<BODY>
Some interesting facts about me.
I like football, cheese and chocolate.
</BODY>
</HTML>
```

What it all means

Go ahead and type this into your editor. The first line of text with all the <!**DOCTYPE**> information in it is something you won't always see in other people's pages, and is not actually required by your web browser. However, what that information does is tell your browser **exactly** what level and standard of HTML you use and how it should be interpreted. This means that as well as looking good in your own particular browser, the information you want people to see will be displayed on just about any browser that there is available in the same way. (Many web pages you will see don't include the details of what version of HTML is being used, and simply use the shortened <HTML> tag to start the document. By using the full DOCTYPE definition, you ensure that you aren't excluding people).

The first thing you will have noticed is that tags are in **pairs** with the first part of the same as the second, except that the second part has a slash (/) before it. This tells your browser that the pair is complete and that the text within the matching pair should be treated in a certain way. Much of the HTML you will use is based on this paired structure (there are some exceptions as we will see). It is important to make sure that, when hand coding HTML, you always close off an HTML tag with the second, matching, part of the pair, otherwise the browser will not know how to understand the HTML properly. You will see how this works in the tags below.

The <HEAD> and </HEAD> tags

These tags allow us to give information about the document itself. In this instance we have given title information within the <TITLE> and </TITLE> tags. Each document **MUST** have a title. Try and make your document titles useful and informative.

The <BODY> tag

The rest of the document is enclosed between the <BODY> and </BODY> tags. In this case, we have a simple sentence.

This is your first and very simple HTML document. and all HTML documents follow this structure. Once you have the idea that this is how HTML works, then the rest is easy.

To view this file, you need to take the following steps

- Save the file to your hard disk as text or ASCII;
- Make sure that it has a simple and easily recognisable name;
- Select the **File** menu from your browser;.
- Select the **Open file** option;
- Find *Myhome.html*, and click on OK.

Figure 3.3 shows this first attempt.

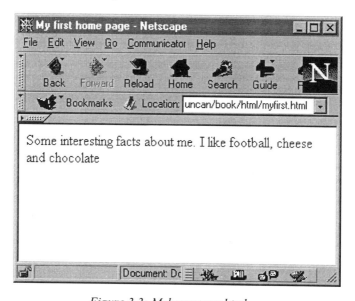

Figure 3.3: Myhomepage.html.

That's it. This is all it takes to produce HTML documents. Admittedly, this page doesn't provide much information, but it is a real HTML document.

How to do more interesting things...

You should now have the general idea about how web pages work, and also that it really is pretty straightforward to put simple pages together. You don't yet have the skills to make your web pages particularly interesting, but you have created your first page. For the moment we're going to concentrate on using the basic tags within HTML effectively and we'll get to the more tricky stuff later.

Commonly used tags

Most HTML documents use about a dozen tags to cover everything. Although HTML is what is describes as a semantic mark-up language—which means that it described the content and not only the appearance—some of the tags which you will use have been developed to control the appearance and layout of your documents.

Using different sized headings; the <H> tags

When your documents start to grow you will need to think about organising the document to make it easy to read. To create sections and subsections in your document you will use the <H> tags, of which there are 6.
The following example (figure 3.4) shows the normal display of the <H1> through <H6> tags as below:

```
<H1>I'm starting big, and getting smaller..</H1>
<H2>I'm starting big, and getting smaller..</H2>
<H3>I'm starting big, and getting smaller..</H3>
<H4>I'm starting big, and getting smaller..</H4>
<H5>I'm starting big, and getting smaller..</H5>
<H6>I'm starting big, and getting smaller..</H6>
```

These <H> tags are typically displayed in diminishing size in your browser. It makes sense therefore to construct your document using the <H1> tag for the title of the document, <H2> as the chapter heading, <H3> as the sections within chapters, and so on.
The <H6> tag is often used to create 'small print'—for example disclaimers or copyright information.

The <P> tag

This is a single tag and in this format does not require a closing tag (though you can include the </P> at the end of the paragraph if you wish. <P> tells the browser that we want to start a new paragraph immediately following this tag. In this simple form, the tag is normally displays as a **line break** (or **carriage return**) in the document.

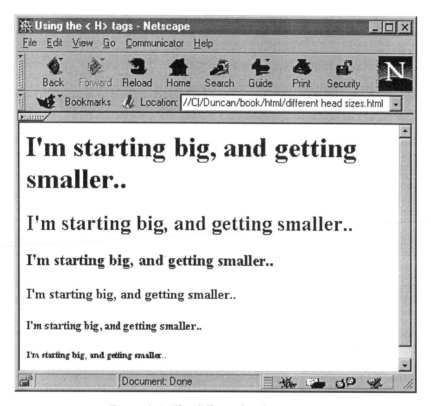

Figure 3.4: The different heading tags.

<P> can take an additional attribute to allow you to set the text alignment for the following paragraph. This is of the form <P ALIGN=RIGHT>, with the default alignment being LEFT (and there is also a CENTER option). When using alignment in conjunction with the <P> tag, it makes sense to close the paragraph with the matching (and most often ignored) </P> tag. Not only does this make the document source easier for you to read, but it can go a long way to preventing the browser getting confused.

The corresponding code looks like this;

```
<P>
Breaking up your paragraphs
<P ALIGN=CENTER>
with HTML
</P>
<P ALIGN=RIGHT>
is dead easy
</P>
```

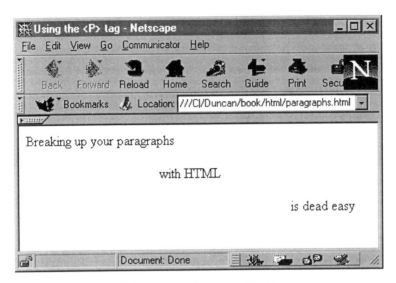

Figure 3.5: Using the <P> tag with alignment.

The <DIV> tag

This tag allows you to chop up your document into sections, without necessarily affecting the formatting of the document when it is displayed; this might not make much sense right now, but <DIV> is a powerful tool for organising your documents, particularly when using   style sheets (see chapter 11). Right now, however, the main use you will have for <DIV> is for shuffling blocks of text around. In conjunction with the *align* attribute, you can shuffle your text left, right and center. Your browser will also normally place a line break after the </DIV> tag.

```
<DIV>I like beer</DIV><DIV>cheese and wine</DIV>
```

produces figure 3.6
The following HTML shows an example of <DIV> to move three sections of text around the screen. Figure 3.7 illustrates this.

```
<DIV align=left>
This is a simple bit of text that is going to be shuffled to the left of the window
</DIV>
<DIV align=center>
Whilst this will be centred, to be closely followed
</DIV>
<DIV align=right>
By this, which is placed to the right of the window
</DIV>
```

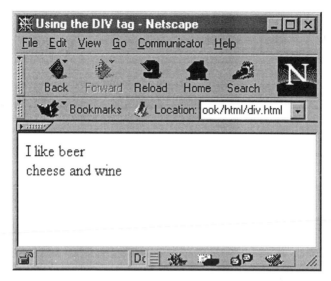

Figure 3.6: Using the <DIV> tag.

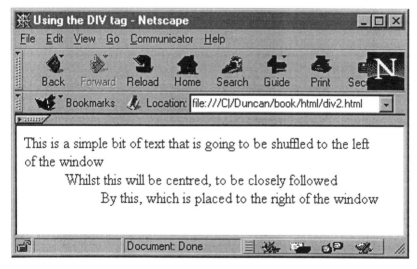

Figure 3.7: Using <DIV> for text alignment.

You should always use the <DIV> tag for text alignment. The commonly used <CENTER> tag has been removed from the specification of HTML, and <DIV> is now recommended in all cases.

The <BR> tag

When you produce a document in HTML, you will quickly become aware that changing the size of the browser window also changes the alignment of the text within it: the wider the browser window, the longer the line of text. To force sentences to end, use the <BR> tag. This tells the browser to break the text at that point, reset itself, and start the next sentence in the default position –the next line down, at the left margin. The <BR> tag doesn't insert any additional white space, whereas the <P> tag usually does. Often the <BR> tag is used when writing, for example poetry, or in this example, witty verse (figure 3.8):

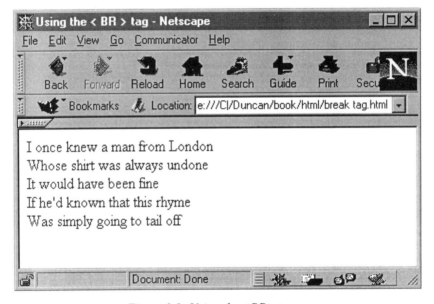

Figure 3.8: Using the <BR> tag

```
I once knew a man from London<BR>
Whose shirt was always undone<BR>
It would have been fine<BR>
If he'd known that this rhyme<BR>
Was simply going to tail off<BR>
```

The <HR> tag

This tag is another standalone tag, for which there is no matching closing tag. It tells the browser to display a horizontal rule across the width of the browser window. In conjunction with the <P> and <BR> tags, <HR> provides us with another straightforward way of breaking up documents. This is the HTML, and figure 3.9 shows the result:

The essence of good HTML<HR>
Is learning the rules<HR>
Then applying them properly

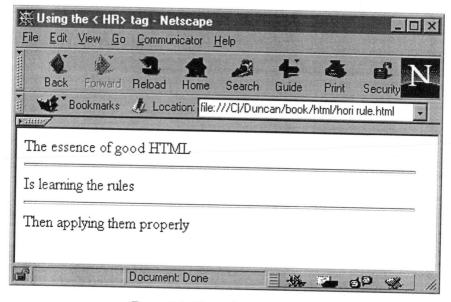

Figure 3.9: Using the <HR> tag.

Structuring your documents

As we noted, HTML allows you to structure your content semantically. The simple tags presented in this chapter provide us with a method of doing just that: headings to tell us how important some of the text is relative to the rest of the document, paragraph tags to logically separate sections of text, and the logical division tag to divide and shuffle text. You will have observed already that most of these tags seem to do very little in terms of what you see in your browser window. However, it is worth getting into good habits now and learn to create well structured documents. It will save you time when your web site becomes more complex.

Coda

In this chapter, we learned to get a browser running, created a couple of files, and used some of the simplest HTML tags to organise text. The next chapter approaches the most powerful tool in HTML: hypertext.

4

Links and Hypertext

Introduction

So far we have looked at simple document structure and how the basics of HTML fit together. In this chapter, we will find out how to:

- Create hypertext links within documents.
- Create hypertext links to other internal and external documents.
- Set up your directory structure.
- Create a hyperlink to other types of information.

More about Hypertext

The *H* in HTML stands for **hypertext**, and it is hypertext linking that is one of the most powerful capabilities of HTML. By using the appropriate tags, you can create 'hot' areas within documents –one click of the mouse can allow readers to jump to other areas of the document. You can also create links between local (other HTML files on your hard disk), and also links to other documents anywhere on the Web. It is hypertext that makes the web a web.

Creating Links

Creating links in HTML documents requires you to use the **anchor** tag <A> (which once again requires its matching closing tag </A>). Use of the anchor tag is slightly more complicated than some of the standard tags we have used so far in that the tag has additional attributes. A typical anchor tag would look something like this:

```
<A HREF="another.html">another document?</A>
```

The attribute used in this case, and the one which you are most often going to use, is *HREF*. This stands for Hypertext REFerence, and tells us where the link points to. In the example above, the HREF is pointing us to another document called 'another.html'.

The text 'Another document' that lies between the opening and closing tags is the area of the document which forms the clickable hotspot: a reader simply clicks on it to jump to the document called 'another.html'. For your browser to jump to this file, it must in this case sit in the same **directory** on your machine.

The term directory simply means where in the structure of all the files of your computer the document sits. Directories (like telephone directories) are just ways to organise lots of bits of information: similar information is grouped into sensible collections so you know where is it.

On computers, directories are organised into **hierarchies**, so that each directory is contained within another one. Therefore the way to locate a file is to specify exactly where in the hierarchy it sits. (This is often referred to as a **pathname** because the way to find a particular file is like going down a path from the start to the end).

An example pathname for a file might be

/hard disk/documents/letters/April/Duncan.html

What this tells us is that the HTML document *Duncan.html* is contained in the directory */April*, which sits within the directory */letters*, which is contained within the directory */documents* which is itself on your hard disk. The slash (/) symbols indicate that what is contained within them is a directory.

If this is confusing try also thinking of the structure of files on a computer as a **inverted tree**: the trunk branches out into successively smaller and smaller branches and then twigs. Following a particular leaf can therefore be found by following a path from trunk, through branches and twigs to the leaf itself.

All this is important because each HTML file sits somewhere on the directory structure of a computer, and to find it you will need to tell the browser exactly where to go. This is especially important in hypertext linking, and for using the hypertext linking tags in HTML. We will see exactly how to specify the pathname of a particular document, and why this is important, in a moment.

HTML files which sit on your own computer (or on the computer which runs your browser) are **local**, and so don't require much additional information to allow you to refer to them. This is because HTML assumes that files which have no full pathname are in the **default** directory - usually the one where your browser is (or one which you have told the browser to use as a default).

If you need to refer to a document which is **somewhere else** on your own computer you will need to give HTML a pathname which leads it to the document. This applies to all local documents.

Computers provide some convenient shorthand to refer to directories on your own computer. One of these is **.** (a dot or period) which means the directory a file is contained in (so *./Duncan.html* and *Duncan.html* are the same document).

The other is **..** (dot dot) which means the directory above the   document is in. So, from the directory *April* in the example above, the file *../ May/Peter.html* would refer to the file *Peter.html* in the directory */May* which is contained in the directory */letters* (i.e. the directory **..**, the directory in which the directory April is contained).

Still confused? Don't worry, this is confusing, and is a result of the fact that computers were designed by very weird people indeed. We will see how it works in practice in a moment which should make you less confused.

HTML documents which sit on **another** machine on the Web are **remote**, and obviously need to have the complete URL to tell the browser where to go and look for them. As we saw in chapter one, this is the complete URL which describes which computer the file is on, and where on the computer it is. Just like looking for a document on your own computer's directory structure, the browser will need to look for the document on the remote computer's directory structure, and so needs a complete pathname in the form of the URL which specifies which computer, and which file and where it is in the directory structure. This is just like the difference between internal and external (postal) mail in your office: you only need to put the name of the person and their department for internal mail, but you need to put the full name and address (including street name and region or town) on external mail.

Links to external documents

Having learned how documents are organised and how to create a link to a local document it is easy to see how to create a link to a remote or external document.

The form of the tag is almost exactly the same as that above. However, as this link is not local, we must include the full URL of the document which we are jumping to. the HTML would look something like this:

```
<A HREF="http://www.atestserver.com/files/another.html">

another document?</A>
```

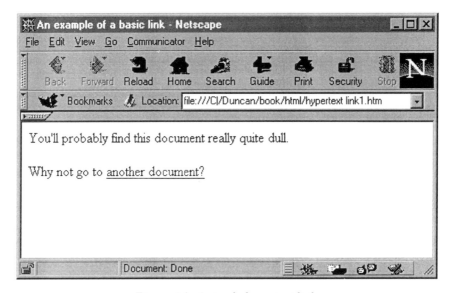

Figure 4.1: A simple hypertext link.

In this instance we are jumping to the website 'www.atestserver.com', going to the files directory, and then opening the document 'another.html'. Even though this document you wish to access could be anywhere in the world this makes no difference to what you see on the browser.

Creating links within the same document

If you have documents that are quite lengthy, reading and remembering all about what is at the top of the document when you are half way down can be difficult. If, for example, you had written an essay using your word processor, it is likely you will have divided the document up into sections and subsections to make for easier reading.

If your essay expands further still into something resembling a book, then you may also consider making a table of contents for the document. This principle can easily be carried over into large HTML documents, where one can create document headings at different levels (as we saw in chapter 3). However, in HTML one needn't stop there we can easily create a table of contents that is active. By simply creating hyperlinks between the items in the table of contents and the sections of the document, we can jump around the document with ease. Let's follow this through as a worked example.

The Soccer Web

One of us is a soccer fan (the other loathes football) and is putting together a web site that gives some information about a favourite club and the players. We collected data about all the players, and decided initially to create a single document with a table of contents. This contents list will consist of a set of hypertext links to jump to the relevant places in my single document.

Here's some of my sample data:

Newcastle United Football Club—Team and Club Information
Management
    Kenny Dalglish
    Terry MacDermot
    Tommy Burns

What we have here is a fairly sensible way of organising the information: indeed if we were producing a handout or information booklet, then this is precisely how its table of contents would appear. Also, for each name in my table of contents we have a short biography. As we shall see, it is a fairly simple task to put this into HTML.

Below is a snippet of the code you would require to form the short table of contents seen in figure 4.2. The other mark-up tags within this example aren't particularly important to what is being illustrated here as they are simply being used to make the output easier to read on the browser.

```
<BODY>
<H2>Newcastle United Football Club-Team and Club Information</H2>
<P>
<STRONG><A HREF="#Management">Management</A></STRONG>
<P>
<A HREF="#Kenny">Kenny Dalglish</A>
<BR>
<A HREF="#Terry">Terry MacDermot</A>
<BR>
<A HREF="#Tommy">Tommy Burns</A>
<P>
```

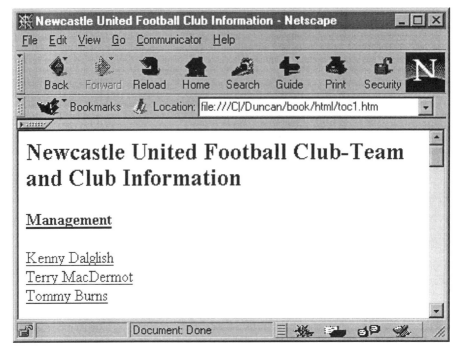

Figure 4.2: Table of Contents.

Following is the HTML to match that above—the **targets** to which the links point.

    <H3><A NAME="Management">Management<A></H3>

    <P>

    <H4><A NAME="Kenny">Kenny Dalglish</A></H4>

Kenny was one of football's greatest ever players, being a key member of the Liverpool team which won every major domestic and international football honour in a ten year period through the seventies and eighties. Retiring from playing, in his first season as manager of Liverpool FC Kenny brought the Championship and the FA Cup home to Anfield. He won the Championship as manager of Blackburn Rovers, and since moving to Newcastle has strengthened the squad ready for next season's challenge in the European Champion's League.

    <P>

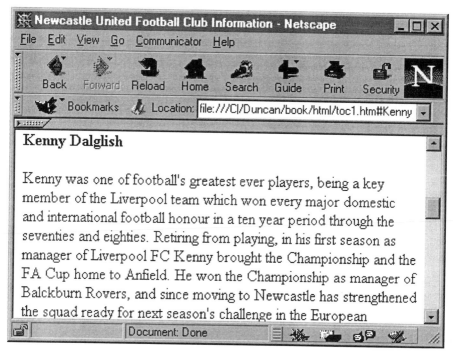

Figure 4.3: Target text.

Looking through the HTML it should be quite easy to spot what is happening here. An area of the document has been declared as a *target* with an entry further up the document referencing that target. The hypertext reference is declared using the *#name* attribute, which tells the browser to look for another anchor within this document taking the name `name`. To reinforce this we'll show the matching snippets of code together. So, the anchor that references the target:

```
<A HREF="#Kenny">Kenny Dalglish</A>
```

and the target referenced by the anchor:

```
<H4><A NAME="Kenny">Kenny Dalglish</A></H4>
```

This simple matching pair of tags is an effective way to make longer documents easier to navigate. However, if your document grows much further it may well become rather annoying having to scroll back up the document to the table of contents. This problem is easily solved by creating the reverse of what we saw above: simply create an anchor that references the table of contents or the document heading as its target. The addition of this tag goes a long way to making larger documents easier to use.

Making it into a 'proper' web

Making tables of contents in the manner described above is not a problem if you only have a few medium sized documents on your site. However as we said earlier, your web site will grow and it makes sense to apply some of the design principles mentioned earlier in the book. Taking the example above, what happens if we want to expand my site to include biographies of all 28 players, some historical information about the club, transfer news or lists of results? You can see that quite quickly this would if kept in a single document become unmanageable not only for the user, but for you as the webmaster.

Right now is the time to go back to your site and perform some system management in order to put a suitable directory structure in place for your site. For this example, we have created the set of directories shown in figure 4.4:

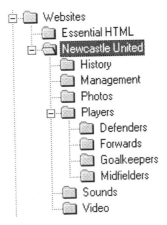

Figure 4.4: An example directory layout.

A simple layout like this can solve all sorts of site management problems and allow you to update the various sections quickly and easily.

Relative referencing: links to other files on your server

This leads us to discuss a slightly different kind of hypertext referencing: **relative referencing**. What we have seen so far is **absolute referencing**: giving the full pathname for each document. Relative referencing allows you to dispense with using the full URL for each document, image or other information you wish to hyperlink to and allow HTML to do some of the work for you with its knowledge of how files are organised on computers. It means that, as we discussed earlier, HTML allows you to provide only the bare minimum of information to refer to the location of each document. The format for relative referencing is like this.

```
<A HREF="../Players/Forwards/Shearer.html">Alan Shearer</A>
```

Here you are telling the browser to step back through the directory structure to the directory above (the shorthand is .. as we saw earlier) and then proceed down through the directories to find the file called 'Shearer.html' which is contained in the directory **Forwards** which is itself contained in the directory **Players**.

This relative referencing is the most common way of navigating through links on your home site as there is no requirement for you to have the full URL every time.

Accessing other forms of information

As we discussed in chapter 1, not everything that is available on the Internet is designed solely for use on the World Wide Web.

However these other sources of information are available to you through your web browser and you can create hypertext links to them in the same manner as creating links for web resources.

The other main source of information is material available via the file transfer protocol or *ftp*. The URLs for accessing material by ftp through your browser look exactly the same as web URLs.

    <A HREF="ftp://ftp.atestserver.com">Jump to my ftp site</A>

This creates a link to an ftp site. Your browser allows you to click on files and transfer them via ftp through your browser window.

Using *mailto*: you can create a hyperlink which when activated opens up your mail program window, inserts the address of the person you want to mail to, and then allows you to send a message. This technique is commonly used at the foot of pages, to allow people to mail the webmaster with any comments or queries they may have, like this:

    <A HREF="mailto:someone@atestserver.com">Mail me</A>

Coda

Creating hyperlinks on your site is easy, but many sites overdo it a little with dozens of links per page. Remember the site design principles we discussed earlier, and particularly the need to keep navigation through the site simple. You should only use hyperlinks when you really need them—don't hang them onto your web site like decorations on a Christmas tree.

5

Logical and Physical Mark-up

Introduction

This chapter shows you how to make changes to the appearance of your text but more importantly, changes to the **definition of your content** in terms **of semantic mark-up**.

In this chapter you will learn about:

- The difference between logical and physical mark-up.
- Which tags to use when, and why.

Use Logical Mark-up!

As the title of this section suggests this is exactly what you should do, and it important to understand the differences between **logical** and **physical** elements of HTML. We suggested in chapter 1 that HTML describes the content of your document, and not the form, and once again this is illustrated through the use of physical and logical mark-up tags. This will be important when we come to chapter 11, when we discuss the use of style sheets.

Using logical elements in your HTML gives you a far greater flexibility and greater chance of 'future proofing' your documents than physical mark-up. To illustrate the point, let us take the <EM> tag versus the <I> tag.

Both of these tags are used in the normal way, with closing </EM> and </I> tags to delineate the selected text. A simple sentence using these tags respectively within an HTML document would look like this:

```
<EM>A brief sentence whose content is emphatic.</EM>
<I>Another whose content is italicised.</I>
```

When displayed on the browser, this is what we see:

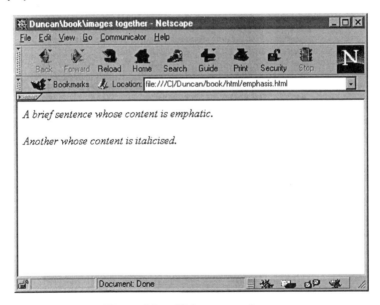

Figure 5.1: <EM> versus <I>.

You will have noted that the two sentences are rendered in exactly the same way—both looking like italic text. In this instance this is indeed the case; however this is only because the browser software can actually produce italic text. Some systems may not be able display italics. Furthermore, the use of a tag such as <EM> allows changes in language usage style to be catered for. As an example, what if in the future the display of emphasised text is commonly acknowledged to be a backward sloping text? The <EM> tag simply says **emphasise** this text **in whichever way is deemed appropriate**, whilst the <I> tag tells us that the chosen section of **text must be italic**. This illustrated the difference between logical and physical mark-up: while physical mark-up only addresses the **appearance** of content, logical mark-up addresses the **semantics** (or intended meaning and use) of content.

More logical mark-up

In the design and implementation of any complex web site—anything more than a few pages—you will need to use many of the logical and physical tags. As we have illustrated above, some of the tags you will use will appear to do the same thing to your text. However, not all browsers and systems have the same capabilities and one of the key design principles is 'reaching everyone'. Using the logical elements in HTML also gives greater potential for you to extract data from your web pages and use them somewhere else.

<CITE>

The <CITE> tag is used when you are citing some material from a reference. It is a standard tag which does not require any attributes. Its syntax is as follows:

```
<CITE>Essential HTML Fast </CITE> is a cracker; you must buy it!
```

Most browsers render text contained within the <CITE> tag as italic though some may produce quotation marks around the text. The cite tag may not seem particularly useful at first glance. However, it enables you to search for material contained within those tags in order to create a global list of citations in no time at all. This could be done using some kind of scripting language. Perhaps future browsers will have automatic content-tag detection mechanisms that allow compilation of the citation list without anyone's intervention.

<DFN>

This tag is used when you are defining a term for the first time. It is most often used in well designed sites which have a reasonably technical content. Its syntax is standard, and it requires no attributes.

The use of the <DFN> tags in technical documents can allow the simple production of a comprehensive web site glossary or keyword index:

<DFN>A new term</DFN>

Generally, the <DFN> tag does not make any difference in the way in which the enclosed text is rendered by the browser. The example below gives an example of both the <CITE> and <DFN> tags.

The clarity and relevance of <CITE>Essential HTML fast</CITE> is one of its major selling points for those of us looking to get a foothold on the <DFN>World Wide Web</DFN>

This produces:

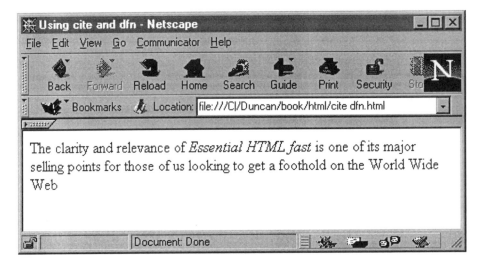

Figure 5.2: The <CITE> and <DFN> tags.

<STRONG>

The <STRONG> tag compares to the physical mark-up element <B> in that in most cases it produces a bold-face font for its enclosed text. Once again however, it provides different browsers with information to use if a bold face font cannot be rendered. Its syntax is as follows:

<STRONG>You must buy this book</STRONG>

<CODE>

The <CODE> tag is used to display code fragments which should appear in a normal paragraph of text. Most browsers render material within the <CODE> tags in a monospaced font—i.e. a typewriter font. It is worth noting that the use of code is only particularly useful for very small chunks of code and normally not more than one line. If you wish to display a section of a program listing, then the code tag is not appropriate, as the spacing is collapsed. The following example illustrates this point:

```
<P>
The use of the following Perl statement <CODE>(useCGI::standard)</CODE>
makes a call to the CGI.pm library. What follows is a chunk of one of the Perl
scripts.
<P>
<CODE>
sub write_form {
        print start_multipart_form();
        print h3("Insert your Username");
        print textfield(-name=>'user_name',
                        -size=>50,
                        -maxlength=>80);
</CODE>
```

Which gives us the illustration in figure 5.3.

As you can see this is effective for the inline code but not particularly useful for the chunk of Perl script. In these instances it is far more effective to use the <PRE> tag which keeps the code in its correct format—see the example in chapter 3.

<INS> and <DEL>

These two tags were introduced to help people with the task of editing HTML documents. They are particularly useful for documents having more than one author, as text to be inserted is simply enclosed within the <INS> tags, whilst that to be deleted is enclosed within the <DEL> tags:

```
<INS>This should be inserted</INS>, and a whole lot more before it's over,
<DEL>whilst this stuff is rubbish</DEL>
```

Unfortunately these two tags are not supported by the major browsers yet, but support will arrive soon, and these useful tags can be tested then.

Physical Mark-up

We have stressed in this chapter the concepts which should guide you in the production of an efficient accessible web site, and the arbitrary use of font mark-up tags simply doesn't help with that aim. However that doesn't preclude the use of physical mark-up tags you just have to make sure they are being used in the correct circumstances.

<I> and <B>

These two tags are probably the most often used, and hence the most often abused. These tags should only really be used in straightforward documents where perhaps it does not matter too much if a particular browser cannot display the tag correctly (the counter-argument is that if it doesn't matter how the text looks then you shouldn't bother using the extra formatting tags anyway). We urge caution in using <I> and <B> arbitrarily as you will make your site difficult to index, reference and display for all users. Use <EM> and <STRONG> if at all possible.

<TT>

This produces text in the teletype font. Once again it is often abused and a source of frustration for designers and users. Often spacing is not preserved correctly for text enclosed within the <TT> tags. Before using this tag, think about the context in which you require things to be displayed in this font. You may find that the content is better suited to using a logical mark-up tag.

<BIG> and <SMALL>

These tags simply enlarge or shrink the size of the text contained within them. They can be nested to make your text progressively bigger or smaller.

<SUB> and <SUP>

Characters can now be set as subscript or superscript to the normally aligned text: This can be helpful for producing elementary mathematical equations.

An example of various physical mark-up tags

The following HTML gives a round-up of various of the physical mark-up tags:

```
<TT>Come on down</TT> to <BIG>Big</BIG> Al's bargain basement.
You'll find all manner of things at <SUB>low</SUB>,
<I>low</I> prices, with <STRIKE>RRP</STRIKE>s slashed.
Be bold, be there, or <B>B</B><SUP>2</SUP>.
```

which produces figure 5.4.

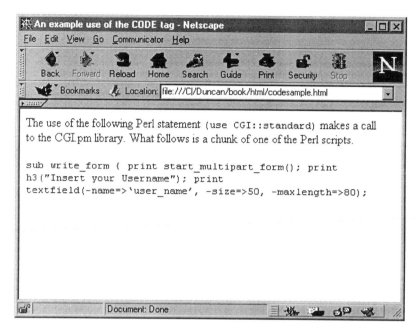

Figure 5.3: Example of the CODE tag.

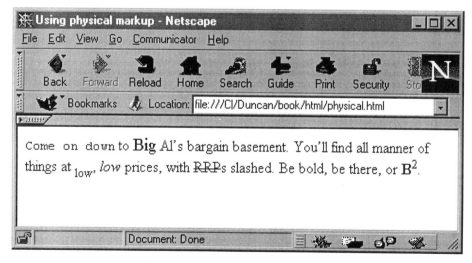

Figure 5.4: Physical mark-up.

Coda

Logical mark-up tags offer a great deal of flexibility in your structured documents whereas the physical styles don't give you any information about the document content. The use of logical styles becomes particularly important when considering the use of style sheets since tags are intended to provide information about the structure of the document.

6

Using Images

Introduction

This chapter addresses the ways to include images on your web site. Using images effectively on your pages is something that can make your web site stand out from the crowd. Specifically in this chapter you will learn about

- Image types supported on the Web.
- Including references to images in your HTML.
- Moving the images around your pages.

The detail in this chapter is   more complex and assumes that you have successfully mastered the basics of page and site construction we have discussed in previous chapters. In particular, we give some technical detail on the creation of image maps and the use of different file types. If you find this confusing, you may wish to review some of the earlier chapters.

Using images

The Web is awash with images and graphics files of one sort or another. As you browse the web you will no doubt have sat patiently waiting for an image to appear in your browser window (leading to the WWW being dubbed the 'World Wide Wait'). You may also have noticed that some web pages download far quicker than others, and this is due to effective use of images within those pages. With a little thought and some patience you can make the images on your web site easier and quicker to download thus sparing your visitors much frustration.

If you work as a designer, perhaps using Photoshop as your professional tool to produce images for the print medium, you will not flinch at the thought of file sizes of tens to hundreds of megabytes (10Mb to 100Mb).

However, when designing images for the web you must bear the following information in mind: a home user trying to download your 10Mb file on a 28.8k modem would have to wait somewhere in the region of **an hour and a half** for the image. This is not ideal.

GIFS, JPEGS and PNG: types of images for the web

The images you see and use on the web right now are going to be one of three types; GIFS, JPEGS and PNG. The two most common file formats are GIF and JPEG. (This state of affairs looks like it may change soon, with the new PNG –**portable network graphic** – file type soon to be supported on the latest browsers). You can use any combination of images on your web pages: JPEGs, GIFs and PNG can happily be mixed and matched since your browser can handle any amount of differing image types on a single page.

GIFS

GIF stands for **Graphics Interchange Format**. Images of this type use the LZW (Lempel-zev and Welch) compression technique, which is lossless; this means that the file size can be reduced without losing any of the file's information. One of the shortcomings of this type of image though is that GIFs can only contain 256 colours (i.e. are 8-bit).

Types of GIFs

Within the GIF definition, there are two different file types; **GIF87a** and **GIF89a**. The former is more usual, whilst the latter offers more functionality – the ability to make areas of an image transparent, for example, which is particularly useful when working with web pages with different background colours or images.

Interlaced GIFs

Interlacing allows the graphic file to download progressively. You've probably seen this on some sites as the images appear quickly at low resolution and then gradually fill in over a few seconds. Again, this can be useful if you wish to allow users to see something of the images on your site very quickly.

When to use GIFs

As a rule of thumb, GIF images work particularly well when you're using cartoon type or flat images and line art. GIFs aren't particularly good with photographic images.

JPEGs

When you work with JPEGs, you can work with 16.7 million colours – i.e. the images are 24-bit but they are still small enough to download quickly over the web. JPEG stands for **Joint Photographic Expert Group**. As the name suggests this file type was developed specifically for dealing with photographic images. The compression technique offers compression ratios of 100:1, and also gives you some control over the amount of quality loss you can put up with your image.

Progressive JPEGs

Progressive JPEGs are a reasonably recent introduction. Traditional JPEGs can take quite a while to appear on your screen, the progressive type appears on your screen quickly at low quality and then resolves into focus.

When to use JPEGs

JPEGs were specifically designed for photographic images so they are best used for smooth, flowing images. Anything that has big colour changes or lettering with sharp edges doesn't look particularly good as a JPEG.

Including images in your pages; the <IMG> tag

To include an image in your page, use the following tag;

<IMG SRC="URL">

where "URL" tells us where the file resides on your server. So, for example, if you have a separate *images* directory on your server with a file called *somefile.gif* in it, then the HTML to include that image would look like this

<IMG SRC="../images/somefile.gif">

You will almost never use an image on a page on its own: your images will be themed around the textual content of your pages. Balancing the appearance of the images you use with the text within the document to create an aesthetically pleasing page can be quite tricky, mainly because of the number of the many additional attributes the <IMG> tag can take. We will discuss these further in a moment.

Alternate text

Believe it or not, some browsers still cannot see images—although admittedly not many people use such browsers nowadays. However, sometimes in the process of downloading a web page images will not appear properly on the page. This may seriously affect the user's ability to read the page and gain useful information from it.

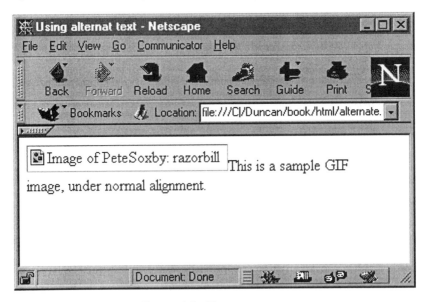

Figure 4.1: Alternate text.

A simple way to at least give the user an idea of what the images would be is to use the ALT attribute. This allows us to define some text which gives us a description of what the image is.

Using this attribute would give the IMG tag the following format:

```
<IMG SRC="petesoxby.gif" ALT="Image of PeteSoxby: razorbill">
```

So, if your browser cannot see the image, at least we get an idea of what should have been there since readers will see the words Image of PeteSoxby: razorbill in their browser.

Moving your images left, right and centre

Shuffling your images around left, right and centre is achieved through the use of other standard HTML tags in conjunction with the IMG tag.

Images appearing on a line of their own are automatically aligned left with the <DIV> tag allowing alignment to the left, center or right of the page. The following HTML produces what you can see in figure 4.2:

```
<HTML>
<HEAD>
<TITLE>Simple GIF image alignment</TITLE>
</HEAD>
<BODY>
<P>
<IMG SRC="peteseoxby.gif">This is a sample GIF image,
under normal alignment.
<P>
<IMG SRC="petesoxby.gif">
<BR>Now with the text appearing below.
<DIV ALIGN=center><IMG SRC="petesoxby.gif"></DIV>
<DIV ALIGN=center>Here it is again centred</DIV>
<P>
<DIV ALIGN=right><IMG SRC="petesoxby.gif"></DIV>
<DIV ALIGN=right>And also right justified</DIV>
</BODY>
</HTML>
```

The Align attribute

The ALIGN attribute controls the alignment of the image with respect to the text being displayed on the page. The attribute takes certain values like this:

```
ALIGN=left|right|top|middle|bottom
```

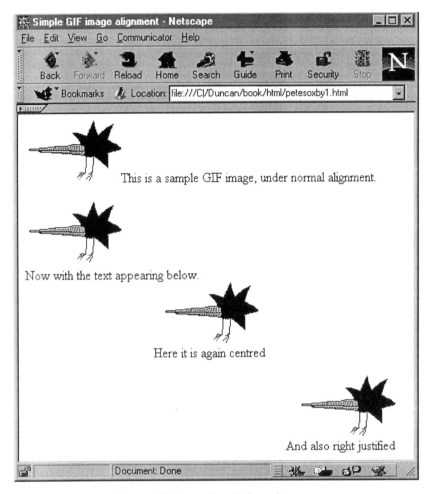

Figure 4.2. Examples of aligned images.

Using a value of 'left' or 'right' will make the image line up against the left or right edge of the page, with the text flowing around it. Using the values of 'top', middle and bottom let the browser know where to put the text which follows the image. To force text below such an aligned image, use BR with the CLEAR attribute. The values TOP, MIDDLE and BOTTOM specify where any text following the image should be put. If more than one line follows after the image, it will be put below the image.

Many of the attributes that can be taken by the <IMG> tag can be substituted by effective use of the <DIV> tag.

The Height and Width attributes

The HEIGHT and WIDTH tags allow us to sensibly scale our image to the size we wish it to appear in our browser. Using the following HTML we can make the image an exact size in mm.

Whilst being extremely useful for fine tuning the size of the image, we wouldn't recommend using the height and width tags to reduce huge images to fit your pages, as unfortunately this always results in loss of image quality. However, they are very useful additional attributes, and take the form, within the image tag:

```
<IMG SRC="PETESOXBY.GIF" HEIGHT=50mm WIDTH=50mm>
```

So, for example, the following HTML:

```
<IMG SRC="PETESOXBY.GIF" HEIGHT=75mm WIDTH=100mm>
<BR>
<DIV ALIGN=center>
<IMG SRC="PETESOXBY.GIF" HEIGHT=100mm WIDTH=125mm>
</DIV>
<P>
<DIV ALIGN=right>
<IMG SRC="PETESOXBY.GIF" HEIGHT=50mm WIDTH=50mm>
</DIV>
```

gives us our same page, with the images scaled in size, as you can see below in figure 4.3.

Using the HEIGHT and WIDTH tags with percentage values, or outlandish values may well cause your browser some problems; Netscape will attempt to display the image appropriately resized, but other browsers may not be so forgiving, and simply will not display the image.

You should be able to see that the quality of the image varies depending on the size we have given it.

The most useful thing about using the HEIGHT and WIDTH attributes is that they allow the browser to gain information about the HTML page layout before it is displayed. Therefore, including these attributes is recommended in all cases, as they result in the textual information of your web pages being laid out very quickly.

In order to use these attributes properly, simply note the dimensions of your image at normal 1:1 scaling in your graphics package, and use those in the HEIGHT and WIDTH definition.

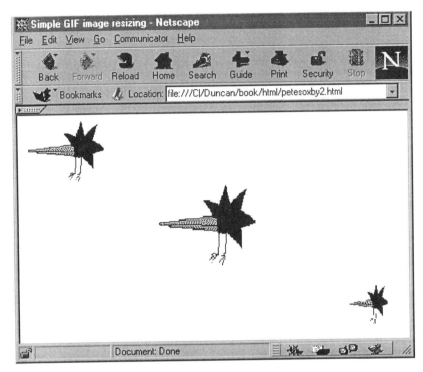

Figure 4.3: Examples of scaled images.

HSPACE and VSPACE

These are two useful attributes to the <IMG> tag which allow us to define an area around the image that is free space. The attributes take a simple numeric value, which defines the number of pixels of free space around the image.

In your page designs, you may often want to use a series of buttons to appear as a button bar. However, with straightforward <IMG> definitions, you run into an alignment problem where the images all run up alongside each other. For example, the HTML

```
<IMG SRC="PETESOXBY.GIF" HEIGHT=50mm WIDTH=50mm>
<IMG SRC="PETESOXBY.GIF" HEIGHT=50mm WIDTH=50mm>
<IMG SRC="PETESOXBY.GIF" HEIGHT=50mm WIDTH=50mm>
<IMG SRC="PETESOXBY.GIF" HEIGHT=50mm WIDTH=50mm>
```

would simply give us the images laid out hard against each other. However, using the HSPACE and VSPACE attributes like this:

```
<IMG SRC="PETESOXBY.GIF" HEIGHT=50mm WIDTH=50mm HSPACE=6
    VSPACE=6>
<IMG SRC="PETESOXBY.GIF" HEIGHT=50mm WIDTH=50mm HSPACE=6
    VSPACE=6>
<IMG SRC="PETESOXBY.GIF" HEIGHT=50mm WIDTH=50mm HSPACE=6
    VSPACE=6>
<IMG SRC="PETESOXBY.GIF" HEIGHT=50mm WIDTH=50mm HSPACE=6
    VSPACE=6>
```

gives us the four images laid out with a 6 pixel space around each of them, both horizontally and vertically. The two different examples are shown in figure 4.4.

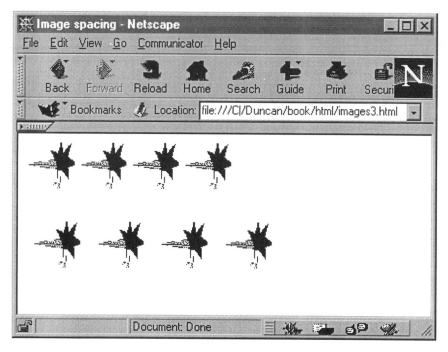

Figure 4.4: Spacing out your images.

Borders

The BORDER attribute is used when the image is a link. It indicates that the browser should draw a border of the indicated size around the image to show that it is a link. Using BORDER=0 turns off borders which is useful since many designers do not like their images to have a border round them. This has the disadvantage that the image content must make it very clear that it's a hyperlink. Figure 4.5 shows an image that is also a hyperlink with its default border present.

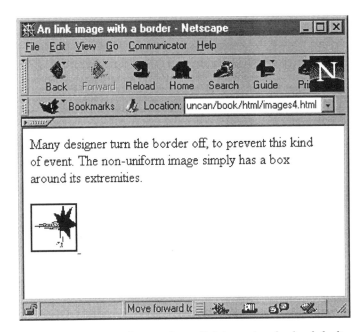

Figure 4.5: An image that is a hyperlink has a border by default.

Client side image maps

Image maps can be useful if you want to use a single graphic as a link to different information: a typical example of this would be a map of a country with its states being separated hypertext links which, when pressed, take you off to some information concerning that state. Image maps are more since the action you can specify is not limited to simple linking: one could, for example, create a hot spot that executes a program.

To create an image map one associates an object with a specification of sensitive geometric areas on that object. Here, we discuss **client-side image maps** (there are server-side image maps too, but they won't be discussed in this book).

A client side image map relies on the browser to interpret the actions carried out by the user (be aware that many older browsers will not be able to handle client side image maps).

Interacting with a single image that has several different possible actions increases the level of complexity of the page design. You must be very careful to make sure that the image that you use as a map is clear and it is obvious what will happen when the visitor clicks on parts of the image.

Creating a map using the <OBJECT> tag

The first step in creating an image map is to create an object that inserts an image:

```
<OBJECT data="imagemap.gif" usemap="#map1"></OBJECT>
```

Using the *usemap* attribute, an association is created between the object and the *name* attribute of the <MAP> tag, by giving both attributes the same value"

```
<MAP name="map1">
```

the next step is to create reference areas which point to other HTML documents, thus allowing you to jump to those documents:

```
<AREA href="newdoc.html"
       alt="Document to jump to"
       coords="0,0,58,58">
```

here, we have defined the area, and given it an instruction to jump to the file *newdoc.html* when activated (as usual there is alternate text for people who cannot view images; the image map may well still work, and in this case, the alternate text becomes a hyperlink).

Finally, the *coords* attribute defines the co-ordinates of the particular mouse-sensitive area of the image.

Button bars

As your site becomes ever more complex, you should find yourself thinking more about usability and navigation issues. It is so easy to let your site become disjointed and inconsistent. One way to get around some of these problems is to have a consistent **button** or **navigation bar** appear on each page on your web site.

The use of a button bar can serve to ensure that there is always access to key information on every page. A simple button bar may contain buttons for searching, a links to your home page, or to go to the first page   of a document.

Furthermore, by thinking what kind of image you want to present, you can use images to give your site a serious, professional feel or something a little more light-hearted.

7

Lists

Introduction

A great deal of the content available on the web is of a fairly **linear** nature before insertion of hypertext links. Much of this information takes the form of **lists**: maybe names and addresses, or telephone numbers. In this chapter, you will learn about:

- Unordered lists.
- Ordered lists.
- Techniques for nesting lists.
- Definition lists.

Unordered lists

The unordered list is, not surprisingly, a list of things that don't seem to go in any particular order (e.g. instructions on what tools and materials you'd need in order to build a garden shed).

The following HTML shows an example of an unordered list:

```
Here's a list of tools and materials you need for building your shed.
<P>
<UL>
      <LI>Hammer
      <LI>Nails
      <LI>Wood
      <LI>Roof felt
</UL>
```

which results in figure 7.1:

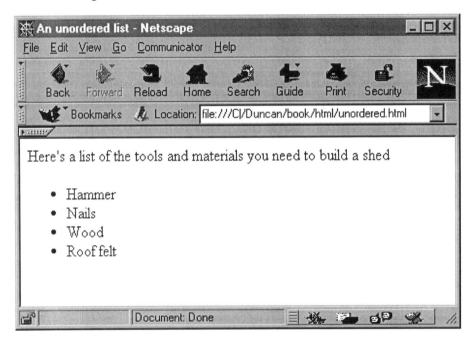

Figure 7.1: A simple list.

The **bullets** are automatically added by the browser and their appearance may depend on the type of browser being used.

Using the type *attribute*

HTML now provides an additional attribute for the <UL> tag—*type*—which allows you to define the type of bullet used before each list item). The type of bullet can be any of: disc, square, or circle. The HTML would look like this;

```
<UL TYPE=disc>
     <LI>One
     <LI>Two
</UL>
<UL TYPE=square>
     <LI>Three
     <LI>Four
</UL>
<UL TYPE=circle>
     <LI>Five
     <LI>Six
</UL>
```

This appears as in figure 7.2.

Ordered Lists

Ordered lists are useful for recounting sequential events—recipes for instance. They are also particularly useful for formatting tables of contents in large documents. The browser formats the list items in the same way as in the unordered list with the key difference being that the list items appear numbered:

```
<OL>
     <LI>Do this first
     <LI>then this
     <LI>and finally....
</OL>
```

Attributes for Ordered Lists

Since ordered lists are numbered there are many more ways of organising the information contained within the list. To cope with this, the <OL> definition can take three attributes: *type, value* and *start.*

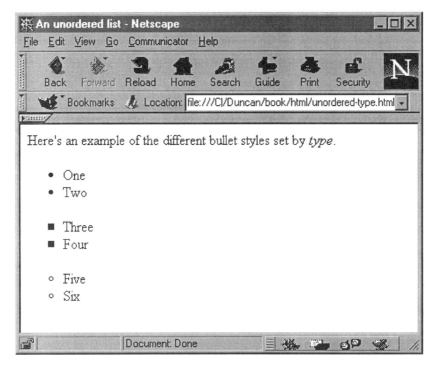

Figure 7.2: Using the type attribute.

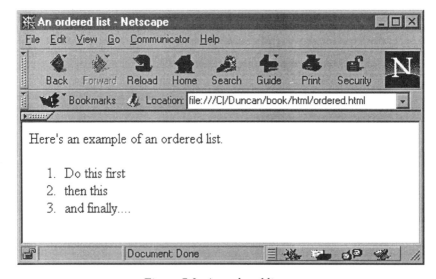

Figure 7.3: An ordered list.

Type

The default way in which browsers number ordered lists is with Arabic numerals (1, 2, 3, 4...). Using the type attribute, the style of numbering can be set:

1 - Arabic numbers (default) (1, 2, 3, 4, ...)

a - Alphanumeric, lowercase (a, b, c, d, ...)

A - Alphanumeric, uppercase (A, B, C, D, ...)

i - Roman numbers, lowercase (i, ii, iii, iv, ...)

I - Roman numbers, uppercase (I, II, III, IV, ...)

A series of numbered lists using the type attribute would appear as in figure 7.4 which has been created with the following HTML:

```
<OL TYPE=1>
      <LI>Do this first
      <LI>then this
      <LI>and finally....
</OL>
<OL TYPE=a>
      <LI>Do this first
      <LI>then this
      <LI>and finally....
</OL>
<OL TYPE=A>
      <LI>Do this first
      <LI>then this
      <LI>and finally....
</OL>
<OL TYPE=i>
      <LI>Do this first
      <LI>then this
      <LI>and finally....
</OL>
<OL TYPE=I>
<LI>Do this first
      <LI>then this
      <LI>and finally....
</OL>
```

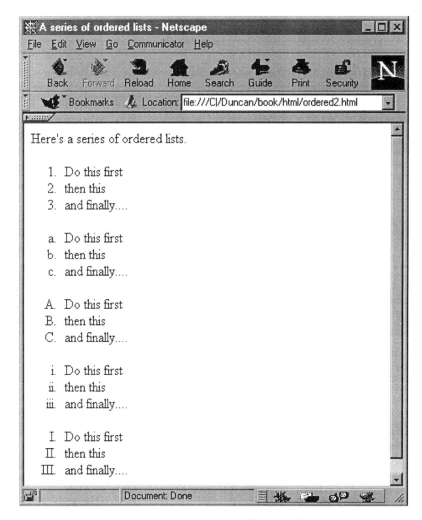

Figure 7.4: A series of ordered lists.

Using start and value

You can start the numbering of your lists at whatever number you like. This is especially useful if you want to break your list to include some extra instructions, then proceed with the list as before:

```
<OL>
    <LI>Hammer
    <LI>Nails
</OL>
```

Remember, hitting your thumb with a hammer can make it very sore; try not to hit your thumb by being very careful.

```
<OL START=3>
    <LI>Wood
    <LI>Roof felt
</OL>
```

which gives figure 7.5.

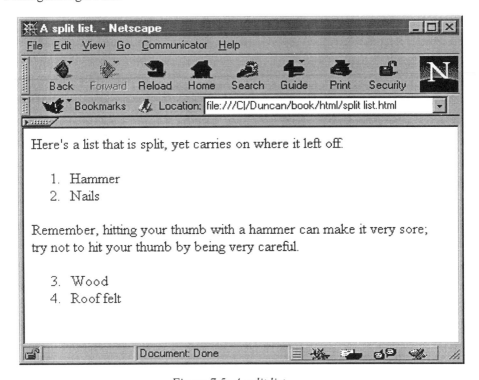

Figure 7.5: A split list.

You can also use *start* and *type* at the same time, defining where you want to begin your list in the style of your choosing:

```
<OL TYPE=a, START=4>
    <LI>I'm starting at the letter D for some reason
    <LI>then proceeding through the alphabet as normal.
</OL>
```

which gives figure 7.6.

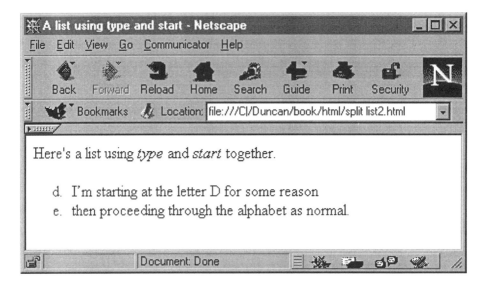

Figure 7.6: Using type and start together.

The <LI> tag

The list item tag is what hangs the lists together, and without it text within the <UL> or <OL> definitions don't show up as list items. So far, we have altered the style of complete lists, using start and type to define the appearance of all the items within the list.

However, the <LI> tag can take the type and value attributes itself to alter the appearance of any number of particular items within the list:

```
<OL>
     <LI TYPE=i>Starting off with lowercase roman numerals,
     <LI TYPE=a>moving to lowercase alphabetic,
     <LI TYPE=I>going through uppercase roman numerals,
     <LI TYPE=1>into Arabic
     <LI TYPE=A>and ending up in uppercase alphabet.....
</OL>
```

giving figure 7.7.

You'll notice that, regardless of the type of character used to order the list items, the progression through from start to end does not change. In this example the fifth list item, which is defined as uppercase alphabetic, is given the 'E' character corresponding to the fifth letter of the alphabet.

Setting values arbitrarily

To alter the number of the list item you can set the value arbitrarily using the *value* attribute. This can be used in conjunction with the *type* attribute to give all sorts of options:

```
<OL>
        <LI TYPE=i, VALUE=10>Starting off with lowercase roman numerals,
        <LI TYPE=a>moving to lowercase alphabetic,
        <LI TYPE=I>going through uppercase roman numerals,
        <LI TYPE=1, VALUE=15>into Arabic
        <LI TYPE=A>and ending up in uppercase alphabet.....
</OL>
```

giving figure 7.8.

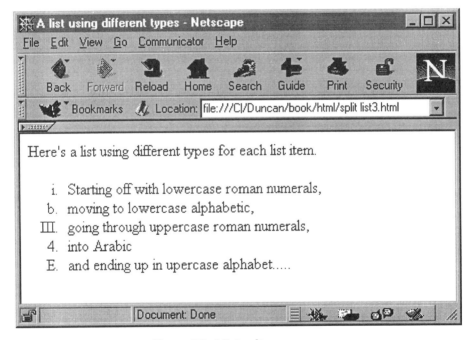

Figure 7.7: Mixing list types.

You can explicitly set any of the values of the various enumeration styles within an ordered list giving a fair amount of flexibility (and also not a little scope for confusion).

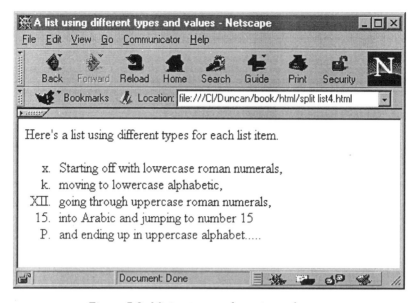

Figure 7.8: Mixing type and starting values.

Nested Lists

In the previous examples, we have shown what you can do with the various attributes available in lists. This flexibility is useful as your lists become more complicated. Lists do not have to operate on a single level—you can make sub lists and sub-sub lists by nesting list definitions inside each other. Each level of nesting adds an indent with respect to the earlier list definition.

Unordered lists

Whilst a sub-level of listing will always produce an indent, the items may not be differentiated from each other in any other way—it simply depends on the browser being used.

```
<UL>
      <LI>I'm at the top of the tree
            <UL>
                  <LI>and I'm on a sub-level
            <UL><LI>and I'm even lower</UL>
            </UL>
      <LI>whilst I'm back at the top
</UL>
```

which gives figure 7.9.

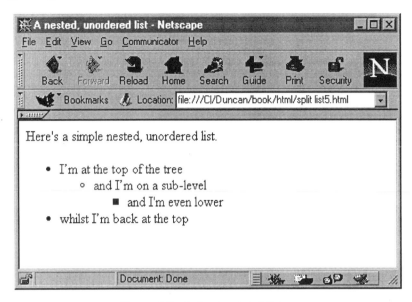

Figure 7.9: A simple nested list.

Ordered lists

Using nesting in ordered lists allows you to separate your tables of contents in a logical orderly manner. Nesting and ordering work perfectly in lists: in conjunction with different item types, you should have all the flexibility you need. The table of contents for one of the authors' lengthy academic book on 'The value of chocolate biscuits in post-modern society' is a prime example:

```
<OL>
        <LI>Introduction
        <LI>Chapter 1:milk or plain, is it an issue?
        <OL TYPE=a>
                <LI>Milk, is it too sweet?
                <LI>Revealing the dark side.
        </OL>
        <LI>Chapter 2: The wholemeal perspective
        <OL TYPE=i>
                <LI>Too crumbly?
                <LI>It's a high fat world
        </OL>
</OL>
```

giving figure 7.10.

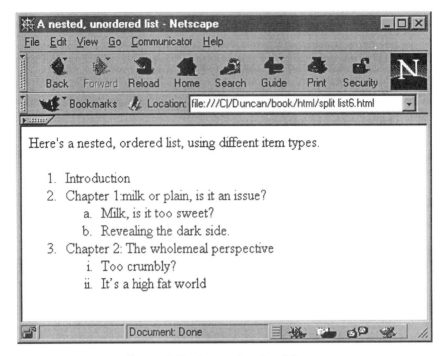

Figure 7.10: A nested, ordered list.

Definition Lists: DL, DT and DD

The definition list is useful for presenting a keyword list, glossary, or any other kind of data that needs defining. A definition list consists of two parts: the term, and its definition. A typical definition list looks like this:

```
<DL>
<DT>Chipmunk
<DD>Small, north American gnawing rodent
</DL>
<DT>Camel
<DD>Large, hump-backed desert animal
```

Each new term in a definition list closes the previous term, so within the <DL> and </DL> tags, no closing </DT> or </DD> tags are required. The above example is shown in figure 7.11.

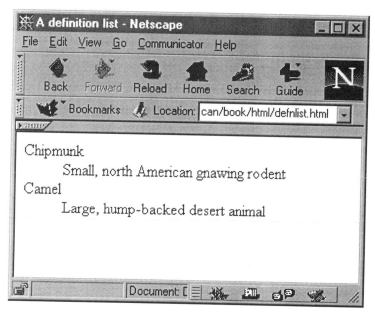

Figure 7.11: A definition list.

8

Forms

Introduction

The introduction of the HTML tags in HTML which allow authors to **create fill-out forms** on the Web is a key development. It allows the development of web sites which don't only display information, but allows visitors to interact the site. Using these tags, authors can create web sites that allow them to, for example, canvas opinion about the design of the site, get feedback on product ranges from clients, and even handle requests and orders. In this chapter, you will learn how to:

- Create the various form elements.
- Design simple and effective forms.

The discussion of forms in this chapter is very basic but you might find it complex: this is because adding this kind of interactive capability to your web pages requires significant ability to both understand the technical foundations of the web and some good design skills.

Form basics

When you need to create a form within your HTML document, you simply define the area to be treated as a form using the <FORM> and </FORM> tags.

Normal text heading, alignment and other mark-up tags can appear within the form definition, but the tags which go to make the active areas of the form cannot appear outside the <FORM> tags.

Whilst the definition of a form is no more difficult than any other HTML mark-up, the process of handling the data sent from the form is far more complicated.

How forms are handled: CGI

The **Common Gateway Interface** is the method most used at present for handling the kind of data you will typically send with HTML forms. The CGI allows you to connect all sorts of other programs to your web pages—for example many sites have large databases which can be queried on-line.

A **CGI program** (or script) is a program which is executed on your web server. The transmission of data from your form causes the CGI script to execute and perform some kind of task. The most common example is the parsing of your form data into something readable, and then storing the data somewhere so that you can access it at a later date.

The use of CGI involves allowing anyone to execute a program on your site which is inherently dangerous, making your site vulnerable to access from unauthorised users. However, there are all sorts of things you can do to make this process a little more secure—this should remain firmly in the domain of your webmaster.

More information about the CGI, commonly used programming languages, and some pointers to several sources will be given in chapter 12.

Defining the form

The <FORM> tag takes several attributes to set up the kind of data that is to be sent; the first of these being the **action** attribute. This is required as your form will not do anything at all unless you have a valid definition of the action attribute. A typical example would be:

```
<FORM action="http://www.atestserver.com/cgi-bin/guest">
```

which means that the data which are encoded and sent in the form are handled by a script called *guest* which sits on *atestserver*, in the *cgi-bin* directory.

Form methods

The GET method

There are two methods by which the data you wish to send are to be bundled up and sent to the server for processing. Historically, the first of these methods was the GET method.

Data sent using the GET method is appended as a string to the URL defined in the form action. This makes data transmitted using this method quick as everything is handled in a single step.

Problems can arise from the use of this method on several fronts. Certain servers can only handle a limited number of characters within the URL being sent for execution and so URLs having masses of form data appended to them using the GET method can quite simply run out of space, chopping some of your data from the end of the string. Thus if your form has many fields, you should be wary of using the GET method. Further, as the data from your form is sent as this simple string, any data which you transfer is particularly vulnerable to being snooped at by any inscrutable network hacker.

The POST method

Used now is the POST method: decoding and dealing with data using the form method is a little more tricky than using GET. However, there are a great many advantages to using the POST method.

It is a two step process and is thus a little slower than GET: first the browser contacts the server and tells it the method of transfer being used, and then proceeds to send the data in a separate transmission. The advantage of this from a security standpoint is that the data within this second transmission can be encrypted before being sent to the server, thus decreasing the likelihood of your data being snooped.

Almost all data from forms is sent using the POST method, and there are a great many useful tools which help you to decode the data. This will be addressed briefly in chapter 12.

Sending a form through e-mail

You can save yourself some bother dealing with forms by simply having the form data sent in an e-mail message—usually to your e-mail address. Perhaps you are renting some space on a commercial server and it is their policy not to allow cgi scripts on their server (this is often the case). Finally, you simply may not have the skills to implement a cgi script with any confidence.

You can, however, use the HTML *mailto* tag to allow you to get at least some feedback from your users. To use this technique, simply include your e-mail address as the action of the form, using the POST method:

```
<FORM action="mailto:jim@mycompany.com" method="POST">
```

This simply sends all the data from the form to your e-mail address. Be warned that, depending on how you have put your form together, the data arriving in your mailbox can be quite messy and difficult to do anything with.

The <INPUT> tag

Most of the input to a form is handled with a variation on the <INPUT> tag. Most of what you would deal with on a normal fill out form—multiple choice lists, tick boxes and text fields—are available within HTML forms, along with several other extremely useful definitions.

The <INPUT> tag defines these fields through the use of attributes which set the appearance of the input fields which the user completes. The standard HTML looks like this:

```
<INPUT type="type" name="name">
```

Further attributes can be defined in order to control the size and shape of the input areas of your form; these will be presented in each example.

Text fields

There are several attributes which allow you to type in straightforward text.

As an example, here is the HTML for a simple form to collect your name and password:

```
<FORM action="http://www.atestserver.com/cgi-bin/script" method="POST">
Please input your name <INPUT type="TEXT" name="user_name"><P>
and finally, your password <INPUT type="PASSWORD" name="pword"><P>
```

which looks like this on your browser (figure 8.1).

As you can see, the input fields are created at a default size, and in the case of the password field, the text we typed into the browser is hidden from view by asterisks. Of course when the form data are sent, the correct information from the password field is also sent.

In this example there doesn't seem to be any way of actually submitting the form data. This is not the case: when you hit the **enter** key the form will be submitted.

However, the first time you are likely to hit the enter key is immediately after having filled in your name in the first text box. You should remember to hit the **tab** key to skip through the fields in your forms; this will save you the annoyance of having submitted partially filled in forms.

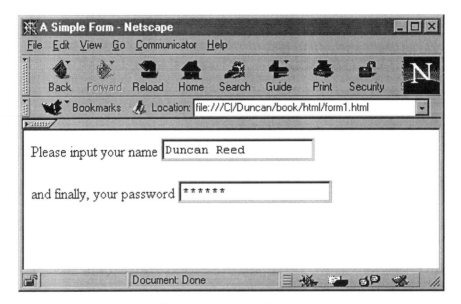

Figure 8.1: A simple form.

Text Areas

The <TEXTAREA> tag within a form allows you to create an area within the form in which the user can type input. This is particularly useful if you're asking people for their comments on a particular question. Its size is defined with row and column attributes:

```
Give us your comments <TEXTAREA NAME="comments", ROWS=3, COLS=20>
</TEXTAREA>
```

Which, in conjunction with the above example, gives us figure 8.2.

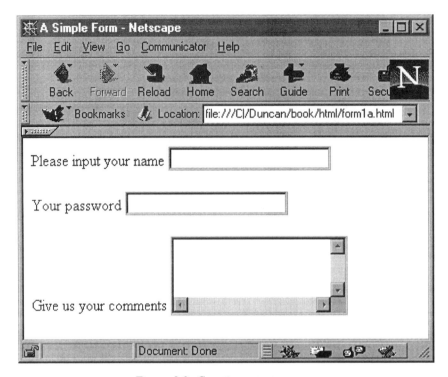

Figure 8.2: Creating a text area.

Creating Submit and Reset Buttons

These two buttons are present on just about every form you will ever see. As their names suggest, these two buttons have the functions of submitting the form, or clearing all the data from the form, respectively.

Following is the revised HTML for the simple form example, with submit and clear buttons included:

```
<FORM action="http://www.atestserver.com/cgi-bin/script" method="POST">
Please input your name <INPUT type="TEXT" name="user_name"><P>
and finally, your password <INPUT type="PASSWORD" name="pword"><P>
<INPUT type="SUBMIT" name="Submit form">
<INPUT type="RESET" name="Clear data"><P>
```

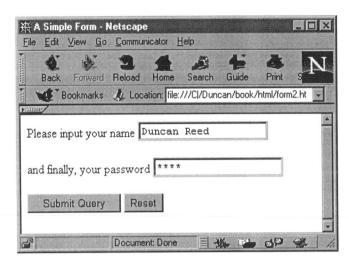

Figure 8.3: Revised form with buttons.

Checkboxes and radio buttons

Checkboxes are particularly useful when creating on-line questionnaires where questions can take several answers. The definition of a checkbox is a simple attribute to be added to the <INPUT> tag:

```
<INPUT type="checkbox" name="answer1" value="True">
```

Note that the checkbox type REQUIRES both a name and a value, to give a matching name/value pair when the form data is submitted. Checkboxes don't mean a whole lot taken out of context and they are far better together in a logical group:

```
<INPUT type="checkbox" name="cars" value="Truck"> Truck
<INPUT type="checkbox" name="cars" value="Van"> Van
<INPUT type="checkbox" name="cars" value="Saloon"> Saloon
<INPUT type="checkbox" name="cars" value="Compact"> Compact
```

You can 'load' the responses in your checkbox group by making some of the values checked by default. For example, you could assume that everyone owns a compact sized car, and to do this, one simply adds a 'checked' instruction in the HTML:

```
<INPUT type="checkbox" name="cars" checked value="Compact">
```

This results in figure 8.5. When the data from a checkbox is submitted, the name/value pairs are what is transmitted. In the above example, the data returned would be:

cars=Compact

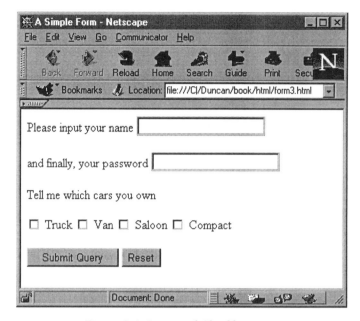

Figure 8.4: Input and Checkboxes.

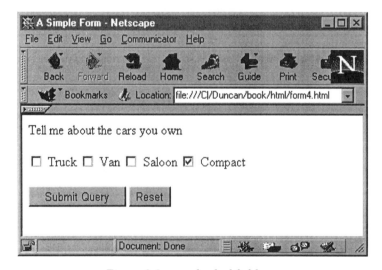

Figure 8.5: pre-checked fields.

Radio Buttons

Radio buttons are used when you want the user to submit a single response from a range of possible responses. They operate like old fashioned car radios: you push one button and the other pops out.

When displayed, one button is always selected from a group of radio buttons. This is the case when the form is first displayed—by default the first button in the group is filled if there has been no specific selection in the form definition:

```
<INPUT type="radio" name="cars" value="Truck"> Truck
<INPUT type="radio" name="cars" value="Van"> Van
<INPUT type="radio" name="cars" value="Saloon"> Saloon
<INPUT type="radio" name="cars" value="Compact"> Compact
```

This provides figure 8.6.

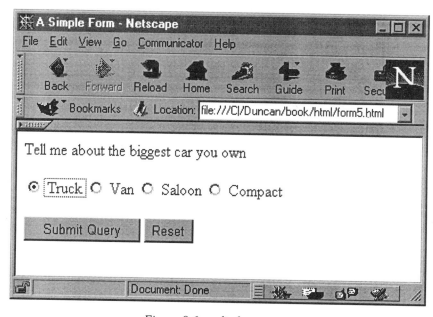

Figure 8.6: radio buttons.

Drop down menus and scrolling lists

You'll be painfully aware how little you can reasonably fit onto one of your web pages and the potential for your web-based forms to rapidly grow even within the simplest of requests. To maximise your 'screen real estate' there are two methods available: **drop down menus** and **scrolling list boxes**. Both use the <SELECT> tag, in conjunction with a number of defined options.

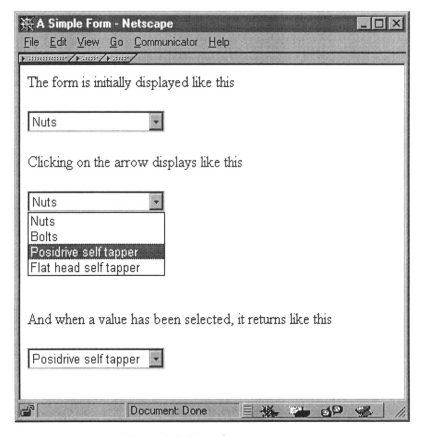

Figure 8.7: Drop down menus.

Drop down menus

The following HTML produces a list of options from which a single value may be chosen:

```
<SELECT>
     <OPTION>Nuts</OPTION>
     <OPTION>Bolts</OPTION>
   <OPTION>Posidrive self tapper</OPTION>
   <OPTION>Flat head self tapper</OPTION>
   </SELECT>
```

which gives us the form layout in figure 8.7.

Scrolling List Boxes

The use of a further attribute gives us the opportunity to select multiple values from our list of options which is displayed on your browser as a scrolling list box. The definition is simple with only the following addition to the <SELECT> definition:

```
<SELECT multiple name="nuts_bolts">
```

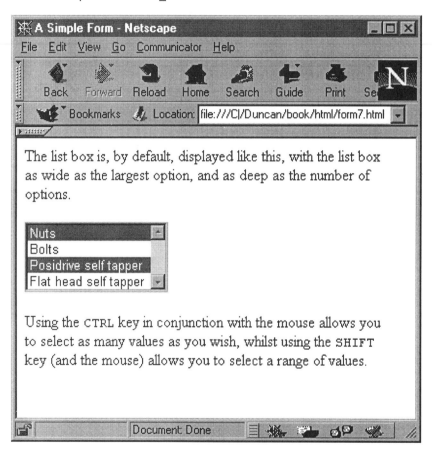

Figure 8.8: Default scrolling list box.

The addition of the options is as before. The result is shown in figure 8.8. This default display is fine for short multiple selection lists but doesn't help a whole lot to preserve screen real estate when you have lots of options to choose from. To deal with this, the

SIZE attribute can be defined in order to keep the list box in sensible proportion to the rest of the form. So, if we now add another eight options to the list, we'll end up with something like figure 8.9:

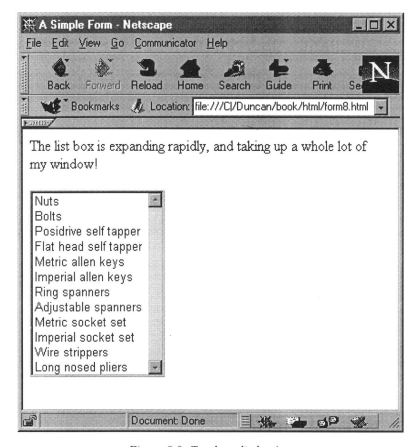

Figure 8.9: Too long listbox!

By using the SIZE attribute we can keep the list box at a sensible size, with four options displayed and the opportunity to scroll through the values using the arrows on the right side of the list box:

```
<SELECT multiple size=4 name="nuts_bolts">
```

This results in figure 8.10:

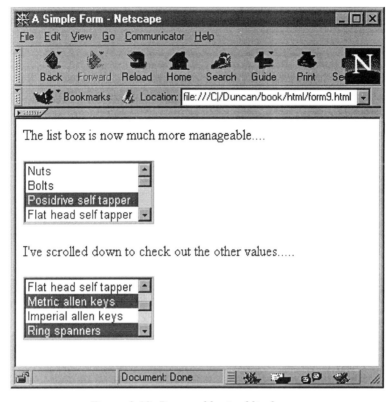

Figure 8.10: Reasonably sized list box.

Coda

The use of forms on the web is hugely popular and there are many ways of dealing with the data that has been sent. A complete treatment of those methods is well beyond the scope of this book and requires a book of its own. Chapter 12 gives some pointers to various associated web programming languages which can be used to effectively deal with forms.

9

Frames

Introduction

Frames were introduced initially as proprietary tags, having been developed by Netscape and have taken some time to become part of the HTML specification. The use of frames must be treated with caution but frames are now very common. In this chapter you will learn about:

- Why frames should be treated with caution.
- The basic frame tags and attributes.
- Making your frame-enabled site useable for everyone.

Designing the Pages

To use frames effectively you must have a very clear idea of what it is that you want to achieve using frames. All too often you will encounter sites using frames as little more than decoration. As we will see later there are many reasons why you should consider alternatives to frames.

Frames split your view of the HTML page up into parts: this moves us away from the atomic view of content on the web—where one URL gives us access to all of the information available on that single page. Splitting views of the content can lead to sites becoming unnecessarily complex in terms of navigation: if one frame in our document contains a hyperlink, then it may change the information in any of the other frames, or even the entire browser window. You must take great care when considering the use of frames on your site. By and large they are hard to implement well, and with the introduction of style sheets (which we will discuss later) not really necessary. Furthermore, frames quite often seem to do horrible things to browsers.

Proceed with Caution

Frames only recently became a part of the HTML standard. in the very recent HTML 4 specification and there are a many reasons as to why you should use frames only in particular circumstances.

The original design of the web provided for all content available to be available on a single page. Frames break this up: you access a page with a single URL, only to be confronted with several sub-pages. This changes the user's view on the content and increases complexity. Readers may now have to perform several different navigation actions to get what they want, rather than the single action that is available in standard pages.

When you navigate through a framed document, the URL may not change with each navigation action, yet your view of the content has changed. This makes the task of **bookmarking** (saving the URL to a bookmark file) quite tricky as the URL does not give a full description of the content available. This upsets one of the fundamental operations of the web—the hyperlink and URL.

Printing from frame documents can also cause problems. When you try to print a document, what will actually be printed? If, for example, you have a scrolling frame on the left with a little information within, and another frame containing the bit you really want to print, what happens to the scrolling frame? Do its margins expand to mimic the layout as shown on the screen?

Frame Tags

Setting up frame documents can be reasonably tricky, but the tags themselves are quite straightforward. A typical definition for a framed page would be:

```
<HTML>
<HEAD>
<TITLE>A sample frame document</TITLE>
</HEAD>
<FRAMESET rows="50%, *">
<FRAME src="doc1.html">
<FRAME src="doc2.html">
</FRAMESET>
</HTML>
```

The content of the frame document is provided by the two normal HTML files, *doc1.html* and *doc2.html* which are written separately, and in this case stored in the same directory as the frameset file.

This example gives us (providing we have the relevant documents, doc1 and doc2):

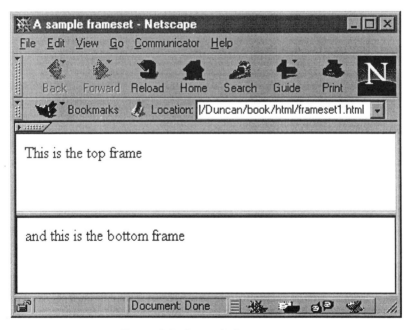

Figure 9.1: A sample frameset.

One of the oddities to notice about the definition of frame documents is that they do not require a <BODY> tag: indeed using this tag will result in your being presented with a blank page.

Frameset and its attributes

The <FRAMESET> tag is the first of the three tags which are required when setting up frames. This tag gives us information about how many frames there are to be in the page, and what the dimensions of those frames are. There are many attributes that can be added within the <FRAMESET> tag, but the principal instructions are the numbers of rows and columns.

As we saw in the above example, the <FRAMESET> instruction was:

```
<FRAMESET rows="50%, *">
```

In this case, the <FRAMESET> tag is taking the single attribute *rows*. Here, we have defined two rows of frames, one taking up a percentage of the browser window (in this case 50%), and the other rows filling the remaining space—in this case also 50%.

Rows and Columns

As you may have gathered, the basic layout of frame document is quite straightforward: the browser window is simply divided into rows and columns by use of the *rows* and *cols* attributes. In the following example, we have divided the screen into four equal parts; two rows and two columns:

```
<FRAMESET rows="50%, *" cols="50%, *">
<FRAME src="frame1.html">
<FRAME src="frame2.html">
<FRAME src="frame3.html">
<FRAME src="frame4.html">
</FRAMESET>
```

which appears like this in the browser (figure 9.2).

Within the <FRAMESET> definition, the <FRAME> references that call the content for the frameset are proceeded through stepwise. Thus *frame1.html* forms the top left frame in the document, *frame2.html* the top right and so on.

There is no real limit on how many frames you can create in your browser window, though common sense should steer you away from defining 50 rows and fifty columns.

Below is an example of a rows-only frameset definition:

```
<FRAMESET rows=25%,25%,50%>
<FRAME src="A.html">
<FRAME src="B.html">
<FRAME src="C.html">
</FRAMESET>
```

Figure 9.3 shows this

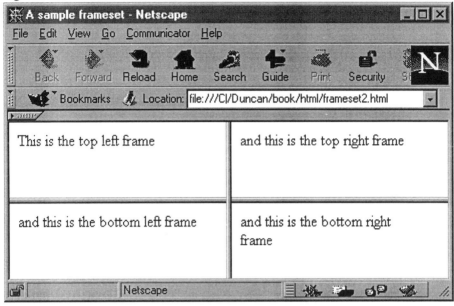

Figure 9.2: Four equal frames.

Nesting frames

Frames can be nested inside each other, to allow you to break specific already framed areas into further parts. The following HTML gives an example:

```
<FRAMESET rows="50%, *" cols="50%, *">
<FRAME src="frame1.html">
   <FRAMESET rows="40%, 50%">
     <FRAME src="frame2.html">
     <FRAME src="frame3.html">
   </FRAMESET>
<FRAME src="frame4.html">
<FRAME src="frame5.html">
</FRAMESET>
```

This provides figure 9.4:

Figure 9.3: A rows only frameset.

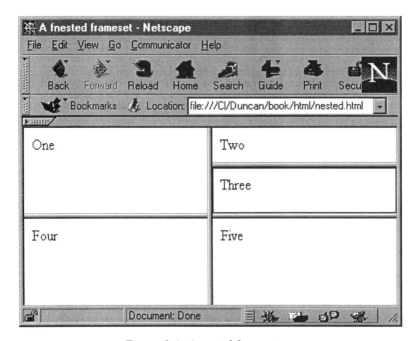

Figure 9.4: A nested frameset.

NORESIZE

When you define the frame display, the size of the frames can be set either by sizes in pixels, or as percentages of the browser window. However, the frame dimensions can be moved around arbitrarily using the mouse. As a web designer, you can prevent this action by using the *noresize* attribute. If you have a two by two frame grid then it should be obvious that by stipulating a *noresize* to any of the frame definitions will result in the frames sizes all being set. The required HTML is shown below:

```
<FRAME src="frame.html" noresize>
```

Scrolling frames

If the content of any of your frames is longer than the window, then the frame definition allows automatic definition of scroll bars. HTML allows you to tweak with this behaviour through the *scrolling* attribute. The scrolling attribute can take one of three values; *auto*, *yes*, or *no*. The HTML would appear like this:

```
<FRAME src="frame.html" scrolling="auto|yes|no>
```

The use of the *yes* value creates scroll bars regardless of whether they are required or not, whilst the *no* value stops scroll bars being created even if the content of the frame is longer than the window space available.

Frame borders

By default the frame definition draws a border around each frame defined, in order to separate the frame from the rest of the document. This behaviour can be stopped using the *frameborder* attribute. The HTML is as below:

```
<FRAME src="frame.html" frameborder="1|0">
```

where 1 is the default value.

<NOFRAMES>

There are still browsers around that can't handle frames, and most of these browsers will simply not display anything when faced with a frameset. Furthermore, some people may prefer to navigate a non-frame interface. HTML caters for this, giving us the <NOFRAMES> tag.

This tag is placed immediately after the first <FRAMESET> definition:

```
<FRAMESET rows="50%, *" cols="50%, *">
<NOFRAMES>
Oops, your browser can't handle this frame page. However, you can
<A HREF="frame1.html">proceed to the first document</A> and navigate
through using the standard interface.
</NOFRAMES>
<FRAME src="frame1.html">
<FRAME src="frame2.html">
<FRAME src="frame3.html">
<FRAME src="frame4.html">
</FRAMESET>
```

We would advise always including the opportunity to skip the frame documents: it doesn't take much coding to do and maximises the potential audience for your site.

Using Frames effectively

Navigation with frames can complex. In our opinion, you should avoid using frames whenever possible. We've given some very good reasons, but there is one main thing you can do to make your frame pages a little more friendly.

The TARGET="_top" attribute

It is very easy to lose track of where you are, and in badly implemented frame sites hypertext links cause a jump to a new place without giving you any idea as to where you are. Since with frames bookmarking that information won't work, to get around this problem, use the TARGET="_top" attribute:

```
<A HREF=somewhere TARGET="_top">
```

When you click this link, the current frameset is cleared, and replaced with a new one, and the browser then gets a handle on where it's at, and bookmarking the URL will now work.

10

Tables

Introduction

Up until quite recently, HTML did not have any real way of dealing with tabulated data. The introduction of the <TABLE> tag and its associated tags has been a boon for content providers, providing a great deal of flexibility in certain areas of document layout. Just about all of the other tags in HTML are allowed to be used within the table definition, further adding to the flexibility and complexity in the use of tables. In this chapter you will learn:

- Simple table definitions: rows, columns and captions.
- Cell spacing and padding.
- Spanning text across multicolumns.
- Grouping of cell data.
- Complex table alignment.

The <TABLE> tag

The <TABLE> tag and its matching </TABLE> tag define the area in your document to be treated as part of the table. To construct a table, you need to define the number of rows and columns and what is to be contained within the cells that are defined by the number of rows and columns. A simple table would look like this:

```
<TABLE>
<TR>
<TD>Some data</TD>
</TR>
<TR>
<TD>Some more data</TD>
</TR>
</TABLE>
```

which looks like this (figure 10.1);

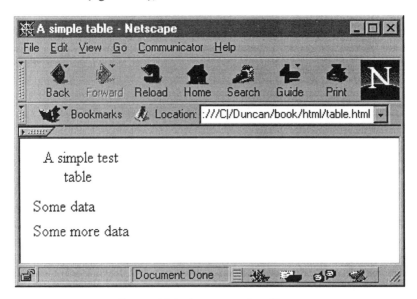

Figure 10.1: A very simple table.

This admittedly doesn't actually look like much more than four lines of text. Because of the simplicity of this particular definition, and the complexity of the table definitions, there isn't much to see. However, we can assure you that this is really a table consisting of one column and two rows.

Adding columns

Adding columns to your HTML is a simple process of adding more <TD> definitions within the <TR> tags:

```
<TABLE>
<TR>
<TD>Some data</TD><TD>Stretching into two columns</TD>
</TR>
<TR>
<TD>Some more data</TD>
</TR>
</TABLE>
```

which gives us figure 10.2:

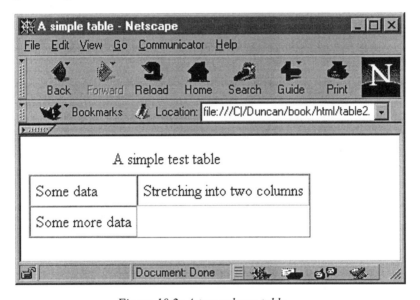

Figure 10.2: A two column table.

You will have noticed the appearance of a border around the table cells. This was done for the sake of clarity, and the addition of the required attributes to achieve this effect will be discussed later.

Captions

Many tables contain a great deal of fairly complex data. It makes sense to add a caption to the table thus giving the reader an idea of what the table data is. Captions are added using the <CAPTION> tag within the <TABLE> definition, and must be placed immediately after the initial <TABLE> tag:

```
<TABLE>
<CAPTION>
A caption for a table about table captions
</CAPTION>
<TABLE>
<TR>
<TD>Table captions line up a caption somewhere</TD>
</TR>
<TR>
<TD>outside the table cell data</TD>
</TR>
</TABLE>
```

which provides figure 10.3:

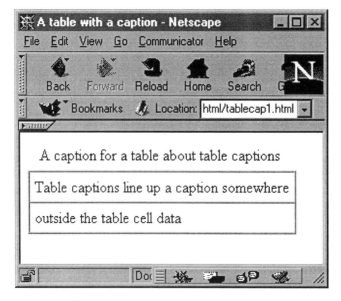

Figure 10.3: A table with a caption.

Alignment with the caption above the table is the default action using the Netscape browser. However, the placement of the caption can be altered using the *align* attribute. This has a number of possible values:

```
<CAPTION align=top|bottom|left|right>
```

This allows you to stipulate that the caption appear at the top, bottom, left or right of the table.

Table headers versus data

The concept of **table headers** should be familiar to you: these are the labels you use in tables to categorise the data held within the table.

HTML uses the <TH> tag and its closing </TH> tag to define the data contained within as being a table header. This allows you to gain information about the type of data within the tag, and most browsers display data from within the <TH> tags distinctly from straight table data.

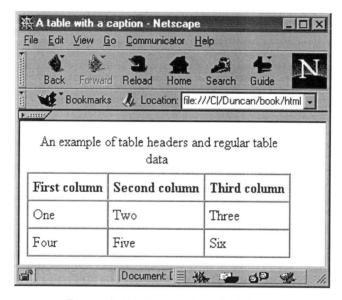

Figure 10.4: Using <TH> and <TD>.

A typical table using table headers and table data would look like this:

```
<TABLE>
<CAPTION>
An example of table headers and regular table data
</CAPTION>
<TABLE>
<TR>
<TH>First column</TH><TH>Second column</TH><TH>Third column</TH>
</TR>
<TD>One</TD><TD>Two</TD><TD>Three</TD>
</TR>
<TR>
<TD>Four</TD><TD>Five</TD><TD>Six</TD>
</TR>
</TABLE>
```

This gives figure 10.4. As you can see, the browser renders the <TH> data in bold, as opposed to the cell data's regular font, which is in a regular weight font.

Borders, spacing and padding

Adding a border

The *border* attribute allows you to define a border around the outside of the table cells. The example below gives a table with a simple border:

```
<TABLE  border >
<CAPTION>
An example of a table with a simple border
</CAPTION>
<TR>
<TD>Aardvark</TD><TD>Badger</TD><TD>Catfish</TD>
</TR>
<TR>
<TD>Donkey</TD><TD>Elephant</TD><TD>Fruitbat</TD>
</TR>
</TABLE>
```

Figure 10.5 shows this.

Spacing

One of the most regularly used attributes to the <TABLE> tag is *cellspacing*. This attribute allows separation of the table cells by simple lines of varying width, that width dependent on the value of *cellspacing*. Adding the attribute to the previous example gives us:

```
<TABLE  border cellspacing=15>
```

Figure 10.6 shows a table with lots of cellspacing:

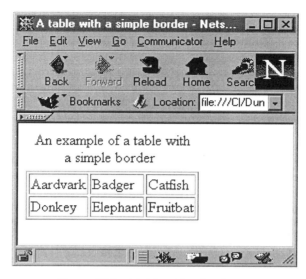

Figure 10.5: A table with a border.

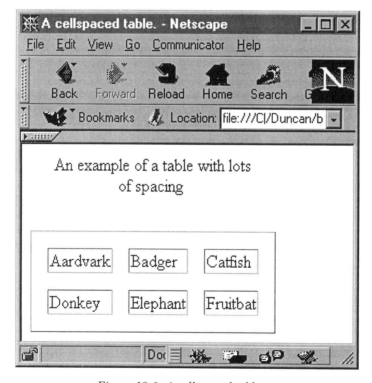

Figure 10.6: A cellspaced table.

Padding

In addition to the *cellspacing* attribute, you can define how much space there is between the cell data and the edges of the cell itself; this is *cellpadding*. Using the same example as above, but replacing the initial table definition with:

    <TABLE border cellpadding=15>

Figure 10.7: A cellpadded table.

Combining all three

These three main attributes of border, cellspacing and cellpadding can be used in any combination, allowing you a great deal of flexibility in your table appearance. You can also produce some pretty monstrous results:

    <TABLE border=20 cellspacing=20 cellpadding=20>

which gives us figure 10.8.

More complex table layout

The opportunities for altering the style and behaviour of your tables are almost endless, and as a result of this it's not practical to give you details of every combination of tags and attributes available. However, there are a great many functions that are particularly useful, and these will be discussed in the following section.

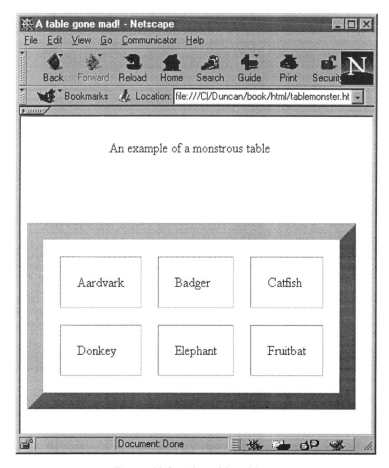

Figure 10.8: A horrible table!

Text alignment in tables

By default, the text that appears in your table cells is aligned to the left of the cell. However, you can choose to align your table data in many different ways. The usual left, right and center, justified, and also you can align the text around a single character:

```
<TABLE  border cellpadding=15>
<CAPTION>
An example of a table with a simple border
</CAPTION>
<TR>
<TH>First column</TH>
<TH>Second column</TH>
<TH>Third column</TH>
<TH>Fourth column</TH>
<TH>Fifth column</TH>
</TR>
<TR>
<TD align=right>Aardvark</TD>
<TD align=center>Badger</TD>
<TD align=left>Catfish</TD>
<TD align=justify>Donkey</TD>
<TD char=n>Elephant</TD>
</TR>
</TABLE>
```

Figure 10.9 shows an example of aligned text.

There is also the facility to move the text around the cell vertically, using the *valign* attribute:

```
<TABLE  border cellpadding=15 height=100>
<CAPTION>
An example of a table vertically aligned text
</CAPTION>
<TR>
<TD valign=top>Top</TD>
<TD valign=bottom>Bottom</TD>
<TD valign=baseline>Baseline</TD>
<TD valign=center>Center</TD>
</TR>
</TABLE>
```

Figure 10.10 shows this.

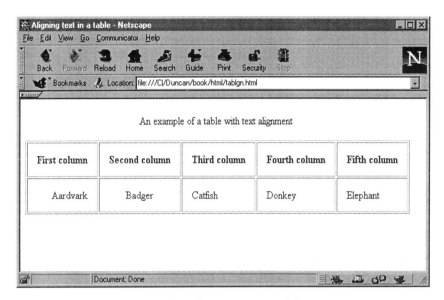

Figure 10.9: Aligning text in tables.

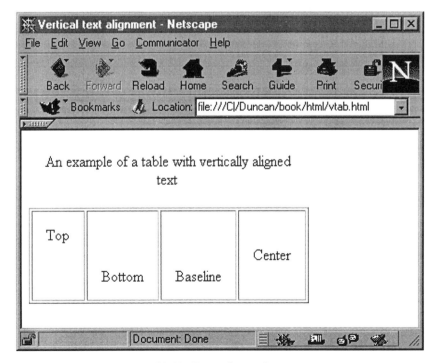

Figure 10.10: Vertical text alignment.

Spanning rows and columns

Often you have table headers or data that covers a range of cells across your table. Spanning across rows and columns is achieved through the addition of the *rowspan* and *colspan* attributes. The example below shows a single header spanning across three columns of data (figure 10.11):

```
<TABLE>
<CAPTION>Spanning rows and columns</CAPTION>
<TR rowspan=3>
<TH>Furry animals</TH>
</TR>
<TR>
<TD>Aardvark</TD><TD>Badger</TD><TD>Cow</TD>
</TR>
</TABLE>
```

Figure 10.11: Spanning across columns.

On larger tables, it may sometimes be necessary not only to span across columns but also down rows:

```
<TABLE>
<CAPTION>Spanning rows and columns</CAPTION>
<TR>
<TH rowspan=3>Furry animals</TH>
<TH>Mammals</TH>
<TD>Dog</TD>
</TR>
```

```
<TR>
<TH>Birds</TH>
<TD>Emu</TD>
</TR>
<TR>
<TH>Insects</TH>
<TD>Tarantula</TD>
</TR>
</TABLE>
```

figure 10.12 illustrates this example.

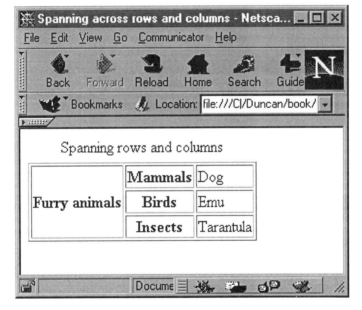

Figure 10.12: Spanning down table rows.

Adding colour

Should you wish, you can now add colours to different parts of your tables, using the *bgcolor* attribute:

```
<TABLE>
<CAPTION>Spanning rows and columns</CAPTION>
<TR>
<TH bgcolor=blue>Furry animals</TH>
</TR>
<TR>
<TD bgcolor=red>Aardvark</TD>
```

```
<TD bgcolor=orange >Badger</TD>
<TD bgcolor=brown>Cow</TD>
</TR>
</TABLE>
```

figure 10.13 illustrates this.

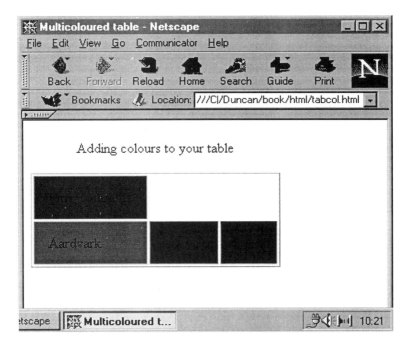

Figure 10.13: Multicoloured table.

Coda

Tables in HTML have an incredibly rich set of definitions most of which have only been briefly covered in this chapter. It is easy to get tied up in knots trying to get various tables to do exactly what you want, but the control you have over layout should be reward for your efforts.

It is worth looking into the use of some of the table tags across your web site: tables can contain just about any other HTML tag so the flexibility is incredible. When you're surfing around you'll see pages with multicolumn layout, with banners across several columns. All these effects are easy to achieve with tables.

11

Cascading Style Sheets

Introduction

Throughout this book, we have talked about the presentation of content in a professional way. One of the key elements in the new version of HTML is the implementation of **Cascading Style Sheets**. Style sheets allow the designer and the user to control the presentation of the web page. The primary advantage is that HTML code can be simple, basic, and adhere to the HTML standard. This makes for happy users—you as a designer can ensure that everyone has access to your documents and the browser-specific troubles outlined previously will simply not matter. In this chapter you will learn:

- The principles behind cascading style sheets.
- How to design your site to incorporate style sheets.
- How to apply style sheets to your site.
- Why you should use style sheets.

Cascading Style Sheets

Cascading style sheets will prove to be one of the most powerful tools available for the web designer. Most people who have used a word processor for any length of time will have come across the principles of style sheets and maybe have used particular style sheets to achieve specific results.

The principle of the cascading style sheet model (or CSS) is no different. Through a style sheet, one can assign all manner of values to our standard HTML tags in order to control the appearance of web pages. With style sheets you can take control over just about every part of your web page: you can specify the amount of white space between text lines, font sizes, font styles, background colours, indents, margins....the list goes on.

Style sheets are also **backwardly-compatible**: using a style sheet will not result in a non-styled browser failing to display the content of your page; of course all the nice formatting you wanted to achieve using the style sheet will not be present, but the user will still be able to see all of the information.

Designing your site for style sheets

Throughout this book, we have laboured to point out the benefits in using the logical elements of HTML to structure documents effectively. The introduction of style sheets to HTML should enhance the structure of your site and should be straightforward.

How style sheets work

A style sheet is a file residing somewhere on your web site consisting of a number of definitions that alter the appearance of your pages. Basically, we can take ordinary HTML tags and assign different display properties to them. Furthermore you can create certain instances of HTML tags that change the tag's style only in particular circumstances.

The basic style definition breaks down into a tag selector and its style definition:

```
tag-selector {property1:value1; property2: value2...}
```

Note that the selector can take multiple properties, each separated by a semi-colon. So to change the appearance of say, an <H1> tag, we would use the following:

```
H1 {font-style: italic}
```

There are several ways of incorporating your style definitions into documents and these methods will be approached later. However, in all cases, your style sheet definitions fall between the <STYLE> and </STYLE> tags, which must appear in the <HEAD> section of your document. The following example of a styled document shows changes in four of the heading styles of HTML:

```
<HTML>
<HEAD>
<TITLE>
Introductory Style Sheet Definition
</TITLE>
<STYLE TYPE="text/css">
        H1 {font-style: italic}
        H2 {text-align: right}
        H3 {font-family: arial}
        H4 {font-style: italic}
</STYLE>
</HEAD>
<BODY>
<H1>Italic first level heading</H1>
<H2>Right aligned second level heading</H2>
<H3>Arial font third level heading</H3>
<H4>Italic fourth level heading</H4>
</BODY>
</HTML>
```

which appears in our browser window like this (figure 11.1);

Inheritance

When you make a definition for, say, the text of your document to be blue, then other definitions within the text will also be blue. Thus if you set the following style for the <DIV> tag:

```
DIV {color: blue}
```

and then a simple text division:

```
<DIV>
Some sample text all in <EM>blue</EM>
</DIV>
```

then the word *blue* is displayed emphatically in blue.

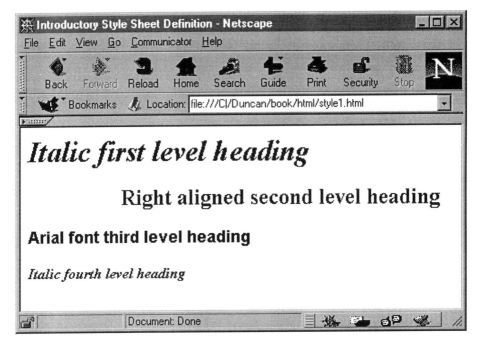

Figure 11.1: A simple styled document.

Context

You can add *context* to your style definitions – a requirement that certain styles only occur under certain conditions

    DIV H3 CODE {color: blue}

This means that anything contained within the <CODE> and </CODE> elements will only be coloured blue if the <CODE> definition is inside and <H3>, which itself must be inside a <DIV>. This carries forward even if there are other HTML tags in between. Thus, the <CODE> would still be blue if there is a <TABLE> tag in between the <DIV> and the <H3>.

Multiple Selectors

If you want to perform a sweeping change across a whole range of tags, then:

    H1, H2, H3 {colour: blue}

makes all <H1>, <H2> and <H3>s appear blue.

Classes

By creating classes we can affect individual tags in our document, giving each tag a style of its own. By hooking into the class attribute available to HTML tags, we can set the style of all the separate blocks of our document. If, for example we have a document like this:

```
<H1>
Chocolate biscuits
</H1>
<P>
Perhaps the best innovation in chocolate biscuit production was the decision to offer
plain chocolate coatings at no extra charge. The slightly more bitter taste of plain
appeals to a great many people who find milk just too sweet.
</P>
```

The style of everything contained within the <P> tags can be altered by defining a class in the style sheet like this:

```
P.aside {font-family: arial, font-style: italic}
```

This is called in the above example like this:

```
<P CLASS=aside>
...stuff about biscuits
</P>
```

Figure 11.2 shows this.

Defining generic classes

Classes can be defined that don't actually belong to a specific tag. This means that commonly used classes can be incorporated in whichever tag you want:

```
.arial {font-family: arial}
```

This creates a generic class which can be included using the class attribute whenever we require it. Thus we could use:

```
<DIV CLASS=arial>
Some text to be displayed in an arial font
</DIV>
```

to make that block of text appear in the specified font.

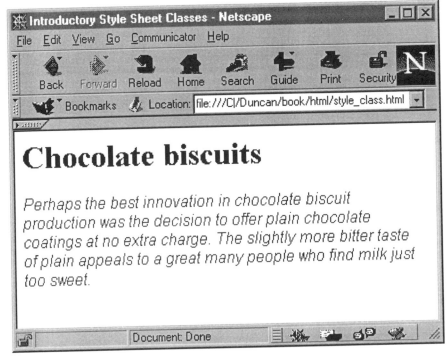

Figure 11.2: Defining a class for a paragraph of text.

Pseudo-classes

There are certain parts of your document presentation that do not depend on the manner in which the document is structured: certain things that depend on a user interaction, for example. The behaviour of hypertext links is one such example.

There are five pseudo-classes available for use, and their names are set; you cannot define pseudo-classes yourself. One can use pseudo-classes to control the appearance of a links' status; whether it has been visited, not visited, or whether it is being activated:

```
A:link {color: green}
A:active {color: blue; font-size: 150%}
A:visited {color: red}
```

This sets the link colours to be green, to change to blue, to increase in size by half when being activated, and to turn red once visited.

One can also use pseudo-classes in conjunction with the <P> tag to control the appearance of the first letter and first line of a paragraph:

```
P:first-letter {font-family: arial; font-style: italic}
P:first-line {font-family: arial}
```

This tells the browser to set the first letter of the paragraph in an italic arial font, with the rest of the first line being in an arial font.

Unfortunately, at the time of writing, pseudo-classes aren't supported by any of the major browsers, so we can't show you their use in action.

Properties

So far, we have defined simple styles for tags using properties seemingly grasped out of thin air. There are, however, a great number of properties defined in the CSS definition and some of these properties will be briefly addressed here. A broader treatment of everything available in CSS is beyond the scope of this text, but chapter 12 provides you with pointers to further information.

Text properties

These properties allow control over such things as text alignment, the amount of space between letters, the amount of space between lines of text, and even the space between words. The following example shows some of the properties in action:

```
DIV.allround {text-indent: 4em; text-align: left; line-height: 150%}
```

Applying this to our earlier treatise on chocolate biscuits gives us figure 11.3:

The text-indent property

This property sets the indent of the first line of the division of text; in this case by a value of 4 *em*s; this is the width of four letter 'm' in the font currently being used. The property can also be set using a percentage; this means that the indent is a percentage of the width of the parent element.

The text-align property

This takes any of four values: *left, center, right* or *justify,* and allows us to shift any block of text around in any of these ways.

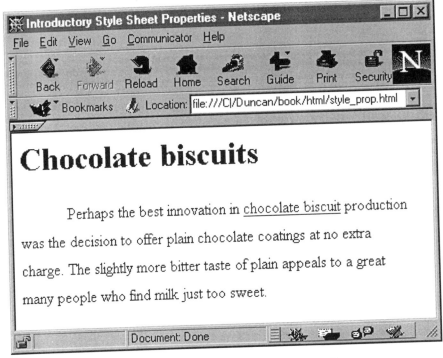

Figure 11.3: changing some of the text properties.

The line-height property

This defines the amount of space between the lines of text in a document. It can take any of four values; relative height, absolute height, a scaling factor, or the keyword *normal*. In figure 11.3, a relative of 150% was used, though an absolute height of, say 10pt, could also have been used:

```
{line-height: 150%}
{line-height: 10pt}
```

Using a scaling factor is different, as the line space is calculated dependent on the size of the font being used at the time. This makes for a uniform display and is recommended in most cases.

Font properties

Using the various font properties really lets you get into the nitty gritty of styling, allowing you to change font styles, sizes and types. You have to take care with mixing all your fonts up though – other people may not have all the fonts available, putting you in a position where your style sheets are not particularly useful. The following example shows various of the font properties available:

DIV.font {font-size: 14pt; font-weight: bold; font style: italic; font-family: arial}

which gives figure 11.4

Figure 11.4: Using font properties.

Colors and background properties

Assignation of background images and colours to each part of your page is also possible using the *background-color* and *background-image* properties:

P.colourful {background-color: grey}
P.image {backround-image: url (images/wavy.gif)}

Note in the image definition the use of the *URL* property, which informs the style sheet to link to the file in *images* called *wavy.gif.*

Linking your style sheets to the documents

There are several ways to link style sheets into documents. Not all of these methods are implemented in the common browsers yet. This should soon be rectified, so we will cover all the methods as laid out in the HTML specification.

Including style definitions in the head of your document

This is the most straightforward way of implementing a style sheet but is only really useful when the formatting you require from your style sheet is quite simple:

```
<HTML>
<HEAD>
<TITLE>
Introductory Style Sheet Definition
</TITLE>
<STYLE type="text/css">
        P.colourful {background-color: yellow}
        P.image {backround-image: url (wavy.gif)}
</STYLE>
</HEAD>
```

Defining a set of styles in the head section of your document quickly results in a messy and lengthy document, making the HTML code difficult to read. It is also not particularly efficient as the style definitions you have made cannot be re-used across other documents.

Linking the style sheets in

Using the <LINK> tag in the document head, you can store your style sheets in a directory elsewhere and call them into your document:

```
<LINK REL=stylesheet HREF=mystyle.css TYPE=text/css>
```

This method allows you to define several possible styles for your documents by including multiple <LINK> tags. Your browser should then present you with a number of possible style sheets available, from which you choose one. The formatting present in that style is chosen, and all the other are ignored. Presently, however, neither of the major browsers support this multiple linking method properly.

Importing styles

This method is similar to the <LINK> method, using, however a special call to a style sheet from within a <STYLE> tag:

```
<STYLE>
@import url(http://www.atestserver.com/styles/mystyle.css);
</STYLE>
```

Once again, however, neither of the major browsers treat this method correctly, so watch out for errors.

Why you should use style sheets

Style sheets allow you to control the appearance of every single file across your web site. You can create themed areas according to the content; different styles for the different sections of your business. The style sheets can be created once and then referenced as many times as you like. The significance of this is that a single change to your style sheet can make changes across every page on your site.

We have mentioned the CSS definition several times so far but the style sheet specification in HTML does not tie HTML to any particular style sheet language. Thus you can pick and choose a language that best suits your needs.

In CSS, the styles can **cascade**: several style sheets can be blended to achieve an overall effect, or if your style is complex you can use multiple style sheets that are physically small in order to make them easier to read.

As we've been at pains to point out, HTML is a language that describes document content. This means that your documents can be **media independent** so HTML pages can be accessed with all sorts of devices such as your PC, a personal organiser, your TV, by speech output devices, or even tactile devices.

Style sheets offer the potential of efficient, well-designed and easily accessible content for the Web.

12

Web Technologies

Introduction

The pace at which the technology in the web world changes is quite breathtaking. New products and techniques are released almost every day, most claiming to be the 'hot new thing'.

The scope of this book has not allowed a full treatment of many of these technologies; after all, we have been trying to give you the essentials of *HTML*. In this chapter, we will briefly look at what we consider to be some of the important technologies associated with the web and HTML. In this chapter, you will learn a little about:

- Multimedia.
- The Common Gateway Interface.
- Perl.
- Java.
- JavaScript.
- Web resources.

Multimedia

Having video and sounds on your web pages is probably one of the coolest things you can do on the web. Unfortunately, effective inclusion of multimedia in your web pages is not particularly straightforward. You must create the sound or movie that you want people to see or hear: this relies on you being able to effectively use often complex software, and there are a variety of different formats (including formats with names such as **MPEG**, **.mov**, **.AVI**, **.au** and **MIDI**) for both video and sound, each with their own considerations. There are problems with file sizes, whether or not your user's browser can display the type of multimedia you want to show, and not least actually including the correct HTML code in your pages.

It is with these considerations in mind that we urge you to treat the use of multimedia with caution. Too many sites have a large amount of ill-thought-out multimedia content that is often uninformative, and causes downloading of pages to be very slow.

Files sizes

Whenever you consider adding multimedia to your pages, the first thing you must consider is the file size. In the chapter about images, we talked about how important it is to try and keep your graphics files small, so that your pages download quickly. Using multimedia takes file sizes into another dimension—it is not unusual for video files to be several megabytes in size, and this may only be a short clip of video. Sound files are often a lot smaller than video, but be aware that a reasonable quality sound clip can still be several hundred kilobytes in size. As a comparison, well designed web pages, with perhaps a half dozen images may only *total* thirty or forty kilobytes in size.

Plug-ins

Actually putting some multimedia content into your pages can be confusing: one of the reasons for this is that there are a great many different sound and video formats around, each having their own way of handling the data that will be downloaded to your machine. Because there are so many formats, most browsers do not handle multimedia automatically. Instead, they rely on the use of **plug-ins**—these are additional pieces of software which 'plug-in' to your browser. Plug-ins are usually designed to allow your browser to handle a specific format, so if you want to be able to view all multimedia formats on your browser then you may well have to download and install a great many plug-ins.

Helper applications

Even if you do not have a plug-in for your browser, you may still be able to see or hear the multimedia. Most browsers allow you to set-up **helper applications**. You

system: by telling the browser to use one of these helper applications when a particular multimedia format has been downloaded, you can still see or hear the sound or video. This does require that you change some of the setting in your browser.

Using the <OBJECT> tag to include multimedia

The <OBJECT> tag is one of the most flexible in HTML as it allows you to include references to any kind of data and instructions to tell your browser what to do with that data. Furthermore, you can include alternatives, so that if your video or sound cannot be played, then at least some kind of information is displayed in your browser. The following example shows the code required to include a movie clip, and instructions to include a standard GIF image if the movie cannot be displayed:

```
<OBJECT title="Billy the wild horse"
<OBJECT data="wildhorse.mpeg" type="application/mpeg">
<OBJECT data="wildhorse.gif">
</OBJECT>
</OBJECT>
</OBJECT>
```

Using the *type* attribute in this example informs the browser of the type of data it is trying to download. If the browser is not aware of that data type—in this case "application/mpeg", then it will not download the MPEG file, and instead display the GIF image "wildhorse.gif".

It makes sense to give the browser alternatives to the multimedia files, in the same way as we give alternative text for standard GIFs and JPEGs: remember, one of the goals of the web is to include everyone.

The Common Gateway Interface

The common gateway interface or **CGI** is the mechanism which allows your web browser to run a program (often called a **CGI script**) on a web *server* and then receive output from the server. The CGI is used extensively in conjunction with HTML forms: data is sent to the web server from the form and fed into a CGI script on the web server via the CGI. The CGI script on the server then processes the data and can pass information back to your browser. The CGI can even be used to connect your database to the web, allowing users to make on-line queries.

CGI scripts can be written in any programming language that will run on a web server: C, Perl and Visual Basic are all used.

There are potential security problems for the web server when using CGI scripts. Essentially you are allowing anyone to run a program on your server, so you must take care when writing CGI scripts. The system administrator will almost always check your scripts over anyway.

Information sent through the CGI is bundled up by the http, along with other information such as what kind of browser the client is running, what the request method was (GET or POST) and what the IP address of the client sending the data is.

If you really want to get into the nitty gritty of how the CGI works, then you can try reading the documentation that came with your web server.

Creating interactivity: programming on the web

There is a great deal of debate about the future of the web, and the place of HTML within that future. As you will have discovered over the course of this book, HTML is quite restricted in some ways. However, we would add that most of the problems arise when attempts are made to use HTML for something for which it was not designed.

People are used to their software being highly interactive, with all sorts of things happening on their screens at once. Standard HTML isn't like that, sure interactivity is facilitated through the hypertext mechanism, but the level of interactivity we see elsewhere is not there. To counter this, the use of programming languages within HTML has arisen, with promises of dynamic, multimedia, all-singing, all-dancing web presentations. Of course the introduction of programming languages increases the level of complexity; one of the beauties of straight-ahead HTML is that practically anyone can get a handle on it.

The information in this chapter isn't intended to be a tutorial, I'm simply trying to give a little background on some of the more complex and new issues appearing in the world of the web

Perl

Perl is an **interpreted** language: in an interpreted language, the program instructions are read line by line by a piece of software which interprets those instructions and then tells the computer what to do. Perl is very often used for writing CGI scripts. The language was originally designed to handle large amounts of simple text, and allow quick and easy sorting and arranging of that text. As most of the information sent via the CGI from web pages is textual, Perl is ideal for this task. Perl has other things going for it: it is interpreted, so any scripts can be checked over by the system administrator for possible security risks, it is available on most machine platforms, and, it is free.

The use of Perl for CGI scripts is very widespread, and there is a huge community of Perl programmers willing to offer help and advice. Many of them even allow you to use programs they've written for free. There are hundreds (if not thousands) of Perl/CGI web sites around, try:

http://www.worldwidemart.com/msa
http://www.perl.com

Java

Even if you've only been surfing the web for a few weeks, it is likely you will have come across Java. Java is a programming language developed by Sun Microsystems, and its main selling point is that it is **cross-platform.** This means that (in theory) programs written in Java should run on any machine, regardless of the type of machine used to write the program.

Java programs are often very small, and thus are suitable for inclusion in web pages. In order to run Java programs (and JavaScript) in your browser, the browser must be quite new. The newer versions of both Netscape Navigator and Internet Explorer are Java aware.

Writing programs in Java is certainly not as straightforward as using HTML. Java is a full-blown programming language bringing with it huge flexibility, and the potential to develop complex applications. The down side to this is that the level of complexity for the ordinary web user increases drastically.

Pieces of Java code to be included in your web pages are called **applets.** The <OBJECT> tag is used to embed the applet within your HTML:

```
<OBJECT classid="java:program.start">
</OBJECT>
```

As we said, compared with HTML, Java is very complex, and programming with Java is not a task to be taken on lightly. However, if you are interested in learning more, the following pointers offer excellent information:

http://www.javasoft.com
http://www.ora.com/info/java/

JavaScript

JavaScript is a language developed by Netscape specifically for inclusion in HTML web pages. The purpose of JavaScript is to enhance the interactivity of the web, and increase the potential for further user interaction. JavaScript can also control Java applets.

JavaScript code is embedded directly into the HTML. This is achieved by enclosing the JavaScript code within the standard HTML <SCRIPT> tag. An example of a simple piece of JavaScript is given below:

```
<BODY>
Some text or other
<P>
<SCRIPT language="JavaScript">
document.write("Some text inserted by JavaScript")
</SCRIPT>
```

```
</BODY>
```

This uses a standard part of the JavaScript language '*document.write*' to insert the message within the parentheses into the web page and thus be displayed by the browser (figure 12.1)

JavaScript can be used to do far more useful things, the above example could have been written in basic HTML. JavaScript can be used to check the data submitted through an HTML form for errors before it is actually submitted to the web server. Clicking on a hyperlink could cause a message window to pop up on the screen.

You may become more interested in the possibilities of using JavaScript as you become more familiar with the web, and want to try your hand at some programming. There are many good sources of information on the web concerning JavaScript, some of which are listed below:

http://home.netscape.com
http://www.webreference.com/javascript/

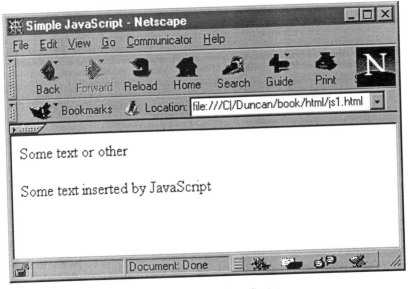

Figure 12.1: Simple JavaScript.

Web resources

Search Engines

Finding information on the web quickly can be greatly aided by using one of the many **search engines** on the web. These search engines hold information about almost every HTML page on the web: you simply type in the words or phrases you are looking for, and the search engine returns a list of possible web sites that may contain the information you want. Some of the best known search engines are:

http://www.excite.com /
http://www.yahoo.com/
http://www.altavista.com/
http://www.webcrawler.com/
http://www.hotbot.com/

The World Wide Web consortium

The development of HTML and all manner of other things to do with the web is overseen by an organisation called the **World Wide Web Consortium** (or W3C). The W3C is an independent body whose aim is to keep HTML and the web open and accessible to everyone. For the most up to date information about HTML, get it straight from the horses mouth at:

http://www.w3.org/

Index

—B—

<BODY>, 23

, 28
<B>, 46
<BIG>, 46

, 29
Browsers, 7, 9
Button bars, 59

—C—

<CITE>, 44
<CODE>, 44
CGI, 76
Client side image map, 58
    Creating a map using <OBJECT> tag,
    59
Clients and Servers, 7
Common Gateway Interface, 76, 123, 125

—D—

<DIV>, 26
<DD>, 72
<DFN>, 44
<DIV>, 54
<DL>, 72
<DT>, 72

—E—

<EM> , 42

—F—

<FRAME>, 91
<FORM>, 76
    Checkboxes, 81
    Creating a text area, 80

Submit and Reset Buttons, 80
Drop down menus, 84
Methods: GET and POST, 77
Radio Buttons, 83
Resizing list box, 87
Scrolling List Boxes, 85
Text Areas, 79
Text fields, 78
Frames, 89
    <FRAMESET>, 91
    Borders, 95
    Nesting frames, 93
    NORESIZE, 95
    Rows only frameset, 94
    Scrolling frames, 95
    Using Frames effectively, 96

—H—

<HEAD>, 23
<HR>, 29
<H1>-<H6>, 24
<HR>, 29
HTML: first page; 22
HTML: head, body and foot, 22
http, 7
Hypertext links 31, 32, 34, 37, 38
hypertext links within documents, 31

—I—

<I>, 42, 46
<IMG>, 51
IMAGES, 49
    As a hyperlink, 58
    Free space around image, 56
    Types supported on Web, 49
    Height and Width attributes, 55
    Alternate text, 52
    GIFS, 50
    HSPACE and VSPACE, 56

Interlaced GIFs, 51
JPEGs, 50, 51
Sizing in mm, 55
Moving images around your pages, 53
Progressive JPEGs, 51
Spacing out your images, 57
<INPUT>, 78

—J—

Java, 123, 127
JavaScript, 127, 128

—L—

<LI>, 68
Definition list, 73
Nested, ordered list, 72
Series of ordered lists, 66
Nested list,70, 71
Split list, 67
Mixing type and starting values, 70
Nested Lists, 70
Ordered Lists, 63, 71
Setting values arbitrarily, 69
Unordered lists, 62, 70
Using type attribute, 63, 64, 65, 125
Using start and value, 66
Using type and start together, 68

—M—

Multimedia, 123
Using <OBJECT> tag to include
multimedia, 125

—N—

<NOFRAMES>, 95

—O—

<OBJECT>, 59
<OL>, 63

—P—

<P>, 25

with alignment, 26
Perl, 45, 123, 125, 126

—S—

<SMALL>, 46
<STYLE>, 120
<SUB>, 46
<SUP>, 46
Search Engines, 129
Style Sheets
Changing text properties, 118
Classes, 115
Colors and background properties, 119
Context, 114
Defining a class for a paragraph of text,
116
Designing your site for style sheets, 112
Font properties, 119
How style sheets work, 112
Importing styles, 121
Inheritance, 113
Linking your style sheets to documents,
120
Multiple Selectors, 114
Principles behind cascading style
sheets, 111
Properties, 117
Simple styled document, 114
Using font properties, 119
Why you should use style sheets, 121

—T—

<TABLE> 98
<TH>,101
<TD>, 101
<TITLE>, 22
<TT>, 46
Tables, 97
Captions, 99
Cellpadded table, 104
Border, 103
Colours, 109
Columns, 99
Text alignment, 107
Vertically aligned text, 106
Cell spacing and padding, 97
Headers versus data, 101

Rows and Columns, 92
Spanning across columns, 108
Spanning down table rows, 109

—U—

<UL>, 62

—W—

Web resources, 129
World Wide Web consortium, 129